APTITUDE, PERSONALITY & MOTIVATION TESTS

APTITUDE, PERSONALITY & MOTIVATION TESTS

ASSESS YOUR POTENTIAL AND PLAN YOUR CAREER

2ND EDITION

Jim Barrett

KOGAN PAGE

London and Sterling, VA

Publisher's note

Every possible effort has been made to ensure that the information contained in this book is accurate at the time of going to press, and the publishers and authors cannot accept responsibility for any errors or omissions, however caused. No responsibility for loss or damage occasioned to any person acting, or refraining from action, as a result of the material in this publication can be accepted by the editor, the publisher or any of the authors.

First published in Great Britain and the United States as *Test Yourself!* in 2000 by Kogan Page Limited
This edition published in 2004

Apart from any fair dealing for the purposes of research or private study, or criticism or review, as permitted under the Copyright, Designs and Patents Act 1988, this publication may only be reproduced, stored or transmitted, in any form or by any means, with the prior permission in writing of the publishers, or in the case of reprographic reproduction in accordance with the terms and licences issued by the CLA. Enquiries concerning reproduction outside these terms should be sent to the publishers at the undermentioned addresses:

120 Pentonville Road
London N1 9JN
United Kingdom
www.kogan-page.co.uk.

22883 Quicksilver Drive
Sterling VA 20166-2012
USA

© Jim Barrett, 2000, 2004

The right of Jim Barrett to be identified as the author of this work has been asserted by him in accordance with the Copyright, Designs and Patents Act 1988.

ISBN 0 7494 4179 8

British Library Cataloguing-in-Publication Data

A CIP record for this book is available from the British Library.

Library of Congress Cataloging-in-Publication Data

Barrett, James.
   Aptitude, personality and motivation tests/Jim Barrett.–2nd ed.
      p. cm.
   Rev. ed. of: Test yourself! 2000
   ISBN 0-7494-4179-8
1. Occupational aptitude tests. 2. Vocational interests–Testing. I. Barrett, James. Test yourself! II. Title.
   HF5381.7.B67 2004
                                    2004002755

Typeset by Jean Cussons Typesetting, Diss, Norfolk
Printed and bound in Great Britain by Clays Ltd, St Ives plc

Contents

Preface

This book was originally entitled *Test Yourself!*, a popular guide published by Kogan Page from 2000 until 2003. Although it was successful, I felt that several improvements could be made, not least to the title, which I had come to see as confusing because it did not specify what kind of testing was involved and what was the intended purpose. I did not want the book to be wrongly perceived as just another games book. I hope that the title *Aptitude, Personality and Motivation Tests* makes the point clearly: while tests can be fun they can also be serious in enabling readers to discover more about their talents and how to use them effectively. Just as importantly I have used the opportunity to restructure the book in ways that I hope will make it easier to use and understand. I have improved some of the tests and added a completely new test to extend the aptitude section even more widely. The aim of this volume is to provide a complete and comprehensive process of self testing and career guidance. I hope it will be useful for people whatever their reasons for wanting to find out more about how their mind works and how their abilities might be applied, for example, to find a career, to plan career change, to develop their potential, to prepare for selection or assessment tests.

Introduction

How to use this book

Aptitude, Personality and Motivation Tests provides you with comprehensive, well-proven, psychological methods that enable you to understand and make full use of your abilities.

If you follow the instructions to each chapter you will be able to build a personal profile of attributes and skills. You can use this knowledge:

- for career guidance, career planning, career development or career review;
- as a preparation for selection or assessment situations;
- for personal awareness and effectiveness;
- to gain insight into the behaviour and personality of others.

Aptitude, Personality and Motivation Tests contains three types of test:

- *Aptitudes.* These are designed to give you information about types of intelligence that are relevant to different skills and careers. Completing all of the tests will allow you to establish your likely strengths and weaknesses in order that you can: 1) know what your strengths are and find a way to use them; 2) know your weaknesses, at the same time not allowing yourself to be limited by them.
- *Personality.* These are designed to help you consider: 1) how your own style may suit some areas of work more than others, which might also suggest how you might 'grow into' or 'move on to' new, different areas of work; 2) how your understanding of behaviour helps you to work with others, who may often be very different from yourself, in order to do your best as team members.
- *Motivation.* These are designed to check out what sorts of activities appeal to you in order to relate these in a structured way to different sorts of activities. These tests should help you select work in which you are going to be interested so that you enjoy what you do.

Each of the chapters contains:

- a test, most benefit being obtained from following the rules for taking the test very carefully, especially the amount of time you should allow yourself where this is appropriate;
- instructions on how to mark the test;
- comments on what the test measures;
- advice on how to use the information from the test.

The tests can be taken in any order depending upon your interest or need.

Testing

The use of tests is increasing. Whether you like tests or not, it is becoming difficult to avoid them. Many employers use them routinely because they find them more reliable indicators of what people can contribute than examination results, or even than someone's experience. For the individual, they can often help establish where opportunities might be available, even though an individual has no previous knowledge or experience of that area.

Here are some of the reasons you might benefit from the tests:

- to obtain some independent advice;
- to become familiar with tests in order to be less apprehensive about them in future situations where you may be 'tested' professionally;
- to gain practice in order that you ensure that you can present your qualities in the best possible light;
- to have a means of comparing your own talents in order to see where you might obtain the most satisfaction in the long term;
- to compare yourself with others in order to make full use of your advantages;
- to better understand that others might have different strengths that could complement your own;
- to understand why you 'get on with' some people better than others;
- to understand why a person may become discouraged or frustrated with what they are doing or who they are working with;
- to better appreciate what examiners or possible employers may be looking for when they use tests;
- for fun.

Your 'hidden' ability

All of us have so much ability that never gets used! In most cases, we are not aware of all we can do. If we are, we may not know how we can best apply it.

People who are happy and successful have learnt to use their ability and, probably, keep rediscovering aspects of it.

There is, of course, no obligation to use your ability. On the other hand, frustration is often an indication that we have ability that we are not using effectively.

All of us go through moments of self-doubt. Perhaps you would like to do something or even behave in a certain way, but are unsure that you could, or think that you would be foolish to try. Often, people ask, 'What might I have become if I had had different opportunities?'

The advantage of objective tests is that they may suggest areas in which you could succeed, even though you have not yet had any experience of them. Also, they may reassure you that you may have a lot more to offer than you might suppose.

If you are failing in a certain area in which the test results suggest you should be doing well, something must be going wrong. Psychologists are used to looking for reasons for misalignment between performance and a person's true ability. Here are some of the common reasons why ability is not always readily obvious:

■   The way you were taught did not suit you. A teaching method brings out the best in one person, but 'turns off' another. Similarly, pupils do better with a teacher they like.

■   Your mental, social or emotional development was not yet ready for you to do your best. In all these areas, people develop at different rates. You might have missed out because you were not ready at the time.

■   Your own attitude worked against you. For all sorts of possible reasons, you chose not to use your ability. Possibly you did not really try because 'there would be no point'.

The timed tests in this book are designed to discover your

ability in an 'abstract' way. That is, the purpose is to test whether you think in a way that has some relation to what you might study as well as to the 'real world' of work.

The assumption is that, *if you have the 'abstract' ability revealed by the test, you have the potential to translate this into something that you can actually do.*

This kind of 'ability' testing is usually called 'aptitude' testing. Other books of mine use the word 'aptitude', which means just the same as 'hidden ability'. It is very likely that this book will at least confirm some of the 'ability' you thought you had. It might also suggest that you have more potential than you thought.

Whilst having everything to gain from 'testing yourself', you have nothing to lose. Tests do not prove that you cannot do something. They can only suggest that you could do something. It is then up to you to do something about it, if you want.

Profile matching

At the end of the book there is a list of careers. Against each career are some tentative suggestions as to how your results on the tests may align with these.

How to do the tests

The aptitude tests

The timed aptitude tests have 'right or wrong' answers. To establish whether there is evidence that you have potential in these areas, they need to be taken in accordance with the instructions provided.

The aim of these particular tests is to make you think about what sorts of problem solving are easier for you and what might be more difficult. This then leads on to a consideration of whether the tests' results can suggest that you would find one area of study or a particular career easier to accomplish than another. Of course, you are not obliged to do what is easiest, and evidence from some of the other tests that look at career preferences might suggest that you are very motivated to achieve at something that you might find comparatively difficult. In the end, is it up to you to decide what will make you feel successful.

You can do the aptitude tests in any order you like. It is not necessary to do all of them, but most benefit is obtained if you do, since you then gain an aptitude 'profile', which shows your strong and weaker areas clearly. This is useful when thinking about applying yourself to work, because most jobs require different abilities in different measures.

Do not get discouraged if you find the tests difficult. They are designed to be so! The intention is to really stretch your mind.

There are more test items than you will be able to do in the time allowed, so the fact that you do not get to the end of the tests does not mean you are not doing well. If you try your best on all the tests, the profile that is produced can give you very useful information about your talents.

Instructions for taking the timed aptitude tests

It is helpful if you test yourself in the strict way that you might experience in other test situations. This will prepare you in the best way for being tested formally for college examinations or for assessments when you seek employment. The following advice and instructions are similar to what you will be told on such occasions:

1. When taking the tests, ensure that you have a place where you can work quietly without interruption. You will need an accurate watch. One that 'counts down' is preferred. Also make sure that the light is good and that you have pencils and rough paper to work on.
2. Read the instructions carefully and do not start until you are clear about what you have to do. This is most important, as you will waste time if you have to turn back to read the instructions once you have already started.
3. You have to do as many items as you can in the time allowed. Do not try to rush through to get everything done. If you do so, you are likely to make mistakes, because the tests have been designed to be almost impossible to finish within the short time given.
4. Work as quickly and as carefully as you can. Try not to guess. On some tests guessing will count against you, so try hard to get the correct answer. (Guessing counts against you in many of the tests you are likely to take during your education and your career.)
5. When you are absolutely sure you are ready, turn over the page and start your time. Stop exactly at the end of the time allowed.

Marking and interpreting your aptitude test results

After you have completed the test, you can check your answers to see how many were correct. Then you can see how well you did by referring to the chart.

Your score will fall into one of five grades, comparing you with other males and females who also took the tests:

ba – below average aptitude compared with most people
av – average aptitude compared with most people
aa – above average aptitude, possibly degree level potential

waa – well above aptitude, at least degree level potential
ea – exceptional aptitude

As you will be comparing yourself with a broad group of people, it is possible you may be comparing yourself unfairly. This could be, for example, because you are younger or older than this broad group who are, on average, about 28 years old. Therefore you might be quicker on some tests, but slower on others, than this group. Some allowance for age is made, as you will see when you come to score the tests. Another example is that of gender, since, on average, females tend to do better than males on verbal tests, whilst males often do better on some spatial tests. However, there are so many different factors and circumstances to be taken into account that you will have to be your own judge as to whether you might be at a disadvantage on any of the tests, allowing yourself some extra marks to compensate if you think that is fair.

How to do the personality and motivation tests

These do not have 'right or wrong' answers to the questions. It is your opinion that counts. You can approach these tests in your own way and take as long as you like.

Other books of mine

Career, Aptitude & Selection Tests is a companion volume to *Aptitude, Personality and Motivation Tests*, and uses similar, structured measures to discover potential that can be useful in planning and developing your career.

Total Leadership is about gaining awareness of how to inspire and motivate people with whom you come into contact.

Part 1

Aptitudes

1

Visual reasoning test

There are two types of problem in this test. In one type, you have to decide which of the objects you are shown is the 'odd one out'. This will be the one that in some way makes it different from the others in the set.

In the second type of problem you are shown a sequence of objects or shapes. Your task is to choose, from the alternatives you are given, the one that would come next in line where there is a large question mark. The examples will show you how to do this test.

Example 1

Which is the odd one out?

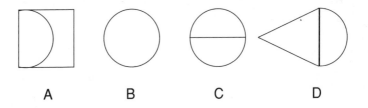

A   B   C   D

Example 2

Which comes next?

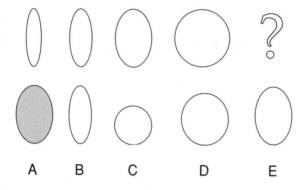

A   B   C   D   E

In Example 1, B is the correct answer. It is the only curved shape that does not also have a straight line.

In Example 2, the figures are of a circle that is turning. The figures can also be seen as a shape that is expanding by equal amounts until it becomes a full circle. The next step would be for the circle to turn by the same amount as before, or to decrease by the same amount as before. E is the correct answer. Although A is the correct shape, there is no reason why it should be shaded. D is not quite the correct size because it has not turned enough. B is not correct because it has turned too much. C is the wrong size and has not turned at all.

You have 10 minutes to do as many as you can. Begin as soon as you are ready.

1.   Which is the odd one out?

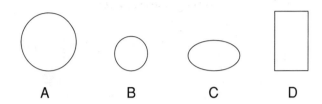

| A | B | C | D |

2.   Which comes next?

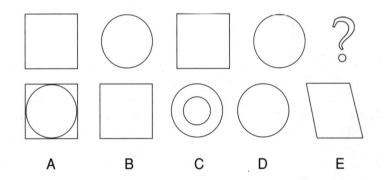

| A | B | C | D | E |

3.   Which is the odd one out?

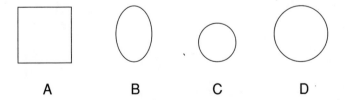

| A | B | C | D |

4.   Which comes next?

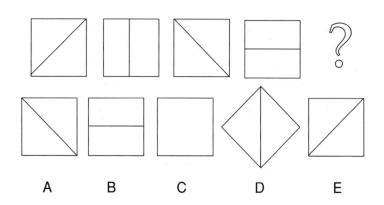

A   B   C   D   E

5.   Which is the odd one out?

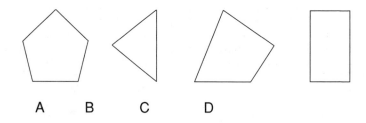

A   B   C   D

6.   Which comes next?

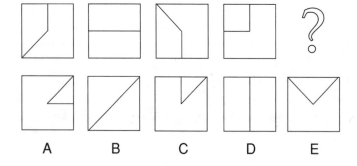

A   B   C   D   E

7.   Which is the odd one out?

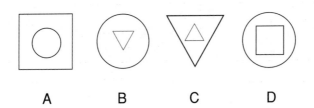

      A   B   C   D

8.   Which comes next?

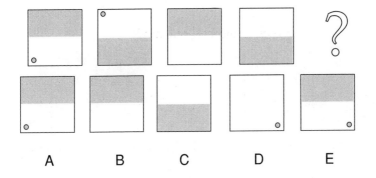

  A   B   C   D   E

9.   Which is the odd one out?

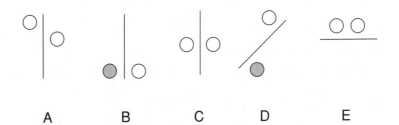

  A   B   C   D   E

10.   Which comes next?

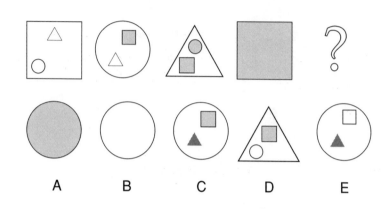

        A   B   C   D   E

11.   Which is the odd one out?

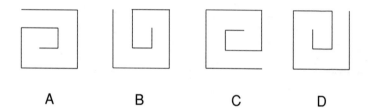

          A   B   C   D

12.   Which comes next?

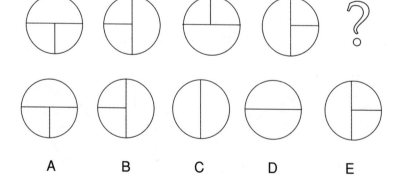

          A   B   C   D   E

13.   Which is the odd one out?

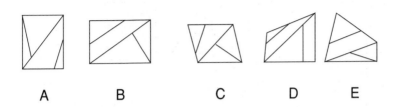

A   B   C   D   E

14.   Which comes next?

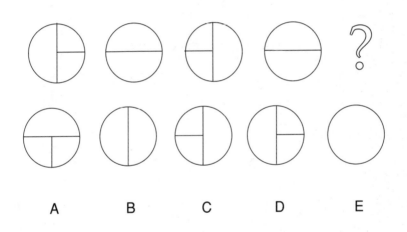

A   B   C   D   E

15.   Which is the odd one out?

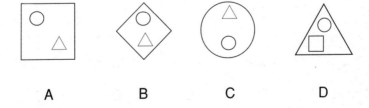

A   B   C   D

16.   Which comes next?

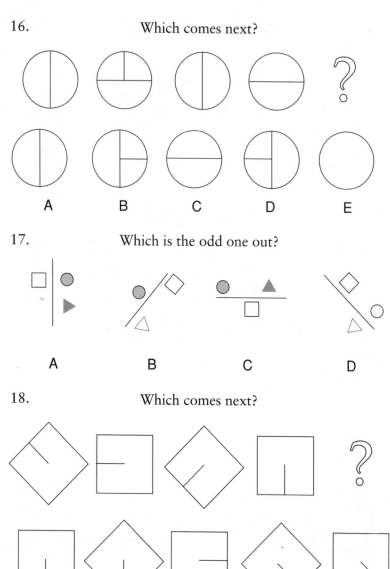

17.   Which is the odd one out?

18.   Which comes next?

19.   Which is the odd one out?

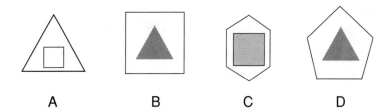

A   B   C   D

20.   Which comes next?

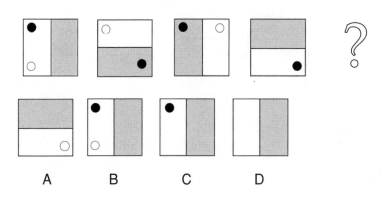

A   B   C   D

21.   Which is the odd one out?

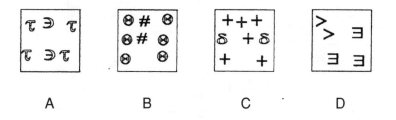

A   B   C   D

22.   Which comes next?

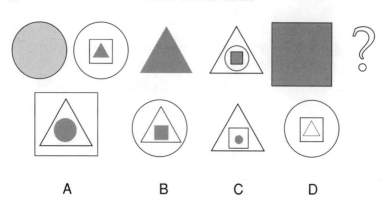

A   B   C   D

23.   Which is the odd one out?

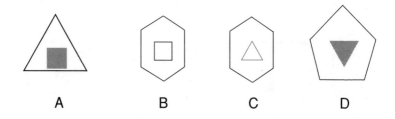

A   B   C   D

24.   Which comes next?

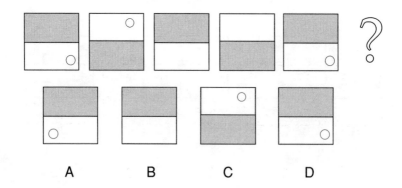

A   B   C   D

25.   Which is the odd one out?

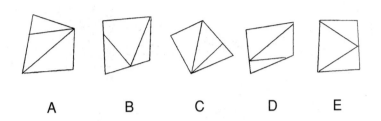

A   B   C   D   E

26.   Which comes next?

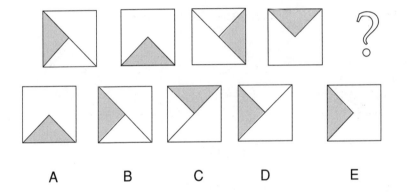

A   B   C   D   E

27.   Which is the odd one out?

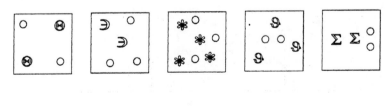

A   B   C   D   E

28.   Which comes next?

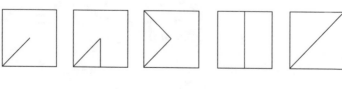

A   B   C   D

29.   Which is the odd one out?

A   B   C   D   E

30.   Which comes next?

A   B   C   D   E

31.   Which is the odd one out?

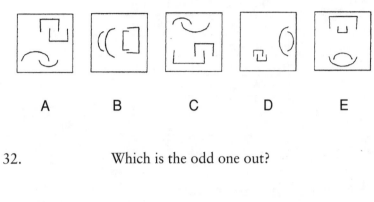

A   B   C   D   E

32.   Which is the odd one out?

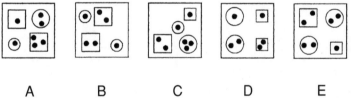

A   B   C   D   E

Answers to visual reasoning test

1 – d	9 – e	17 – d	25 – e
2 – b	10 – a	18 – d	26 – b
3 – a	11 – b	19 – a	27 – b
4 – e	12 – a	20 – b	28 – b
5 – c	13 – d	21 – d	29 – c
6 – c	14 – d	22 – a	30 – d
7 – c	15 – c	23 – a	31 – b
8 – a	16 – a	24 – c	32 – d

Obtaining the total score

	number correct =	_____	
	plus 3 if no mistakes	+3 _____	
	Total score =	_____	

Establishing level of potential

below average	average	above average	well above average	exceptional
1–2	3–7	8–13	14–20	21+

Interpretation

This is one of the tests that is closest to measuring 'natural' intelligence, that is, intelligence that you are born with, rather than abilities you acquired. Although the verbal and numerical tests are also reasoning tests, the ability to read and to work with numbers has had to be learnt. Therefore the visual test is one of the 'purer' measures of aptitude, testing your reasoning with clues that do not have words or numbers. However, it is not the 'best' measure of innate intelligence, since some highly intelligent people do not do well on this test – they may require words or numbers to express their intelligence.

If you do better on the visual test than on the verbal or numerical reasoning tests, it often follows that you have a leaning towards science. When aptitude on the visual test is not accompanied by success on the numerical test as well, the leaning is towards those sciences that are less obviously numerical, such as the biological sciences. When numerical reasoning is also strong, the leaning tends more towards the physical and chemical sciences, as well as technology and engineering. When verbal reasoning accompanies strong *visual* reasoning, the preference is often to move more towards the social sciences.

People who do well on the visual test are often good at detail and at researching information, whether it is in science or in areas such as historical research.

Numerical reasoning test

In this test you are given numbers that connect in some way. They connect along the row, but there is also a relationship with the numbers that are above or below each other. Sometimes a number is missing and a space mark, or line (–), has been put in its place. One of the numbers has been replaced by a question mark (?).

From the information given, you have to find the number that would replace the question mark.

Example 1

1	–	3	?
–	4	6	8

Answer =

The most logical answer is 4; it fits the sequence 1, 2, 3, 4 because a 2 could replace the space mark. Also, 4 is half of 8, in the same way that 3 is half of 6, 2 is half of 4, and 1 is half of 2. The answer, 4, makes all the numbers fit together logically.

1	2	3	4	
2	4	6	8	Answer = 4

Example 2

1	–	9	?	
2	6	–	54	Answer =

The numbers in the lower line are always twice the number in the line above. Also, from left to right, each number is multiplied three times.

1	3	9	27	
2	6	18	54	Answer = 27

Working out the correct numbers for the empty spaces can help you find the number that can replace the question mark. You have eight minutes to do as many as you can. It is important to work as quickly as possible in order to get as many right as possible in the time allowed.

Begin as soon as you are ready.

1.
4	3	2	?	
4	–	2	1	Answer =

2.
2	4	6	–	
4	?	12	16	Answer =

3.
1	?	5	7	–	
–	6	–	–	18	Answer =

4.   –   –   8   4   ?
         64   32   –   –   4   Answer =

5.   2   3   ?   –   13
         –   –   5   8   13   Answer =

6.   3   6   9   12
         9   ?   –   36   Answer =

7.   25   16   9   4
         –   4   ?   2   Answer =

8.   3   7   ?   –
         4   8   16   32   Answer =

9.   7   12   22   –   82
         4   9   19   ?   Answer =

10.   13   14   16   ?   28
         1   –   4   8   –   Answer =

11.   3   7   16   35   ?
         1   2   3   –   5   Answer =

12.   11   14   –   ?
         33   42   60   87   Answer =

13.   3   6   5   8   7   –
       7   11   11   15   15   ?   Answer =

14.   ?   5   7   12   –
       3   –   8   13   20   Answer =

15.   4   5   8   10   ?   20
       10   8   20   16   40   –   Answer =

16.   3   7   5   ?   7   11
       –   4   2   4   2   –   Answer =

17.   5   10   7   12   –
       10   30   ?   60   54   Answer =

18.   6   13   20   –   34
       ?   24   37   –   63   Answer =

19.   0   5   3   13   11   ?
       5   –   10   2   20   –   Answer =

20.   13   ?   22   31   53
       78   45   –   93   –   Answer =

Answers to numerical reasoning test

1 – 1	6 – 18	11 – 74	16 – 9
2 – 8	7 – 3	12 – 29	17 – 28
3 – 3	8 – 15	13 – 19	18 – 11
4 – 2	9 – 39	14 – 2	19 – 31
5 – 5	10 – 20	15 – 16	20 – 9

Obtaining the total score

	number correct =	_____	
	plus 2 if no mistakes	+2 _____	
	Total score =	_____	

Establishing level of potential

below average	average	above average	well above average	exceptional
1–2	3–5	6–8	9–13	14+

Interpretation

The numerical test is much more than a test of arithmetic, since it involves working out the relationship between numbers and detecting a pattern. Although some arithmetical skills are required, the test measures mathematical potential in a broader way than the skill of arithmetic does. Often people who do well on this test say that they have never done particularly well with mathematics, whereas it is only lack of practice involving the 'rules of numbers' – how to subtract, divide, and so on – that has made mathematics difficult for them.

Potential in this area could point to many careers where the analysis of quantitative data is important. Such areas might be as diverse as marketing and science, because both involve the use of statistics. If you have a high score, you would probably readily grasp financial information in business, even though you may be somewhat slow or careless with accounting.

If your score is much higher than those for visual and verbal reasoning, you will probably prefer a career that specifically uses this potential in the first instance. You would probably prefer to follow courses that have a mathematical element, depending upon your motivation. If your interests are commercial, then economics or business studies might suit you. If your interests are more technical, then courses in science, engineering or computing might suit you.

If your score is accompanied by high verbal reasoning, then you might prefer a career where you can use numerical as well as verbal ability, so commerce, business or teaching would be some of the possibilities for you to consider. When your numerical score is accompanied by visual reasoning potential, your leaning is likely to be more scientific or technical, at least at the outset of your career, though your eventual direction will be influenced by your personality.

Verbal analysis test

In this test we are looking at the way you can draw logical conclusions from the information you have been given. There is always sufficient information for you to work out the correct answer. You should not draw upon any previous experience or information you suppose might be relevant. You are given some facts and some possible answers. Tick the letter that corresponds to the correct answer.

Example 1

The town of Newport is further west than the town of Flatpeak, although not so far west as the town of Daybridge.

Which town is furthest east?
Answers: a) Newport   b) Daybridge   c) Flatpeak

The answer cannot be a) because Newport is west of Flatpeak. It cannot be b) because Daybridge is even further west, so Flatpeak must be to the east of both other towns. The answer is c).

Example 2

Fred, Mack and John all have two different cars each. One of them does not have a Ford. Mack is the only one to have a Ferrari. John has a Ford. Fred and Mack have Buicks.

Who has a Rolls-Royce?
a) Fred   b) Mack   c) John

The answer is c). It cannot be a), because Fred has a Ford and a Buick. It cannot be b), because Mack has a Ferrari and a Buick.

Because of the amount of information you are sometimes asked to deal with, it is recommended that you have a piece of scrap paper so that you can, if you wish, draw and make notes or plans. Diagrams, like the following, are often helpful:

	PEOPLE:		
CARS:	Fred	Mack	John
Ferrari	✗	✔	✗
Buick	✔	✔	✗
Ford	✔	✗	✔
Rolls-Royce			

You have ten minutes to do as much of the test as you can. Get your scrap paper and pencil ready in case you need it. Work as accurately and as fast as you can. When you are ready, start the clock and begin.

1. Emma lives further up the hill than Jane. Pauline lives further up the hill than Emma.

   Who lives furthest up the hill?
   a) Emma   b) Jane   c) Pauline

2. All the girls like sports. Sue and Josie like tennis, while Sally and Anne like running. Both Sue and Anne like swimming.

   Who likes tennis and swimming?
   a) Sue   b) Josie   c) Sally   d) Anne

3. Who likes swimming and running?
   a) Sue   b) Josie   c) Sally   d) Anne

4. Mr Everton and Mr Soames have longer holidays than Mr Francke. Mr Porter has a shorter holiday than Mr Francke, while Mr Peters has a longer holiday than Mr Francke.

   Who has the shortest holiday?
   a) Mr Everton   b) Mr Soames   c) Mr Francke
   d) Mr Porter   e) Mr Peters

5. Toby, Rob and Frank all take a holiday by the sea, while Sam, Jo and Tony go hiking in the mountains. Frank, Sam and Jo travel by air. Jo, Rob and Tony do not enjoy their holiday.

   Who goes to the sea and does not enjoy their holiday?
   a) Toby   b) Rob   c) Frank   d) Sam   e) Jo   f) Tony

6. Who does not travel by air and goes hiking?
   a) Toby   b) Rob   c) Frank   d) Sam   e) Jo   f) Tony

7. In reverse order, the most popular holiday tours offered by a travel company are Toronto, Florida, Rome and Paris, although Rome is extremely popular whatever the time of year. After a marketing promotion, Toronto becomes more popular than Rome, but less popular than Florida.

Which tour is most popular after the marketing promotion?

a) Toronto   b) Florida   c) Rome   d) Paris

8. Which tour is least popular after the marketing promotion?

a) Toronto   b) Florida   c) Rome   d) Paris

9. Fred, John, Garth and Joe all have children. Fred and John are the only two to have boys. John and Joe take their children to school by bus, while it is short enough to school for the others to walk. To be fair, Fred and Joe are car owners, and sometimes do use their cars to get the children to school.

Who owns a car, but usually goes to school by bus?

a) Fred   b) Joe   c) John   d) Garth

10. Who does not own a car and has a daughter?

a) Fred   b) Joe   c) John   d) Garth

11. In a museum, Modern Sculpture is to be found on the floor below Watercolours. Greek Pottery is on the floor above the Oil Paintings. The top floor contains the Italian Collection. Watercolours are on the same floor as South American Art, whereas the Oil Paintings are on the floor below Modern Sculpture.

What is to be found on the lowest floor?

a) Modern Sculpture   b) Watercolours
c) Greek Pottery   d) Oil Paintings
e) Italian Collection   f) South American Art

12. Which two are on the same floor?
    a) Modern Sculpture and Greek Pottery
    b) Watercolours and Oil Paintings
    c) Oil Paintings and South American Art
    d) None of these

13. Casey, Stuart, Ritchie, Billie and Colin all buy their own vehicles. Casey and Colin have room for three passengers as well as themselves. The others have room for only one passenger besides themselves. Ritchie and Casey have good front tyres, though the other tyres on all of the other vehicles are dangerous. Casey and Billie have vehicles that take diesel fuel. The others have vehicles that take petrol.

    Who can take three passengers in their diesel vehicle?
    a) Casey   b) Stuart   c) Ritchie   d) Billie   e) Colin

14. How many people have dangerous tyres on diesel vehicles that have room for only one passenger?
    a) 5   b) 4   c) 3   d) 2   e) 1   f) None

15. Who can take only one passenger, but has some good tyres?
    a) Casey   b) Stuart   c) Ritchie
    d) Billie   e) Colin

16. Mrs Booth has difficulty feeding her four children as each one will eat only certain foods. Sharon and Robina will eat rice and lamb. Kelly and Sharon are the only ones who like both bread and cheese. Kelly and Sam both eat chicken and bread.

Which is the only food that Sharon does not eat?
a) bread   b) chicken   c) lamb
d) rice   e) cheese

17. Who eats cheese, chicken and bread?
a) Sharon   b) Kelly   c) Robina
d) Sam

18. Who does not eat cheese, but does eat lamb and rice?
a) Sharon   b) Kelly   c) Robina
d) Sam

19. Which food will be acceptable to most of the children?
a) bread   b) rice   c) lamb
d) cheese   e) chicken

20. Mr Marx's and Mr Bagshaw's cars are black. The others
have red ones. Mr Bagshaw and Mrs Chance have a white
stripe on the sides of their cars. Miss Jenkins has a blue
stripe on the side of her car. Mr Fleming and Mr Marx
have silver stripes on the sides of their cars. Miss Jenkins'
and Mr Fleming's have blue upholstery, while the others
have white.

Who has a car with blue upholstery and a silver stripe?
a) Mr Bagshaw   b) Miss Jenkins   c) Mrs Chance
d) Mr Fleming   e) Mr Marx

21. Who has a car with a silver stripe and white upholstery?
a) Mr Bagshaw   b) Miss Jenkins   c) Mrs Chance
d) Mr Fleming   e) Mr Marx

22. Who has the red car with a blue stripe and matching upholstery?
    a) Mr Bagshaw   b) Miss Jenkins   c) Mrs Chance
    d) Mr Fleming   e) Mr Marx

23. In a basketball competition, Centurions are beaten by Raiders. Saracens beat Centurions. Saracens are beaten by Raiders and Aztecs. Centurions and Raiders are beaten by Aztecs.

    How many games do Saracens win?
    a) 1   b) 2   c) 3   d) 4   e) 0

24. How many games do Raiders win?
    a) 1   b) 2   c) 3   d) 4   e) 0

25. Who emerges as the champions?
    a) Raiders   b) Saracens   c) Aztecs
    d) Centurions

26. Stopping at the shop, on the way to school, Cheryl and Tom are the only ones not to buy chocolate. Of the five children, four of them, including Laura, buy fudge. Unlike the others, Sally, Cheryl and Sandy do not buy any toffee. In fact, Cheryl only buys fruit gums as she does not like other kinds of sweets.

    Who only had a piece of toffee and a piece of fudge?
    a) Sally   b) Cheryl   c) Laura
    d) Tom   e) Sandy

27. Who had three sweets?
    a) Sally   b) Cheryl   c) Laura
    d) Tom   e) Sandy

28. Who are the two people who took the same number and type of sweets?
    a) Sally and Laura   b) Sally and Tom
    c) Laura and Tom   d) Tom and Sandy
    e) Sandy and Sally

29. In total, how many sweets were taken by the group?
    a) 7   b) 8   c) 9   d) 10   e) 11   f) 12

30. Jane, Rachel and Tessa are girls who are wearing a jacket, coat or skirt in blue, green or red. None of these articles of clothing are in the same colour and each girl is wearing something of each colour. The coat belonging to Tessa is not green. Rachel's jacket and Jane's skirt are the same colour. Tessa's skirt is red. Her jacket, Rachel's skirt and Jane's coat are all the same colour.

    What colour is Tessa's coat?
    a) blue   b) green   c) red

31. What colour is Jane's jacket?
    a) blue   b) green   c) red

32. Which girl has the green coat?
    a) Jane   b) Rachel   c) Tessa

33. Which girl has the blue jacket?
    a) Jane   b) Rachel   c) Tessa

Answers to verbal analysis test

1 – c	10 – d	18 – c	26 – d
2 – a	11 – d	19 – a	27 – c
3 – d	12 – a	20 – d	28 – e
4 – d	13 – a	21 – e	29 – d
5 – b	14 – e	22 – b	30 – a
6 – f	15 – c	23 – a	31 – c
7 – d	16 – b	24 – b	32 – a
8 – c	17 – b	25 – c	33 – b
9 – b			

Obtaining the total score

	number correct =	_____	
	plus 3 if no mistakes	+3 _____	
	Total score =	_____	

Establishing level of potential

below average	average	above average	well above average	exceptional
1–3	4–8	9–12	13–17	18+

Interpretation

A similar test, with different items, was also given in my book *Career, Aptitude & Selection Tests*, where it was called 'Critical dissection'. This is exactly the skill it demands, almost as though you have to be a detective, weighing up clues and deriving some logical conclusion from what often appears to be confused. It requires a critical analysis of the facts given, but it also demands that you make logical assumptions about information that can only be derived from what you have been given so far, since vital information is not given to you directly. In this test you need the ability to be able to 'put two and two together'.

In the same way as the other reasoning tests, the verbal test requires you to analyse the situation with which you are presented. The verbal test assesses whether you can reason using words, as opposed to numbers or visual information. If you do better on this test than the other reasoning tests, you will almost inevitably be drawn towards careers where you are involved with communications in some form. High verbal as well as numerical reasoning or visual reasoning is frequently a good indicator of 'academic' potential across the humanities, social sciences and biological sciences.

Obviously, the verbal reasoning test requires some amount of vocabulary, but the complexity of the words themselves is not what is being measured. Often, people whose second language is English do well on this test because they have the logical mind to enable them to achieve with it, even though their level of vocabulary is much lower. It is worth comparing your own score on the verbal reasoning test with the vocabulary test. If you obtain high scores on both, it really does seem that a career involving words and communications would suit you. If you are high on verbal reasoning, but low on vocabulary, you will probably use your ability in talking with people, perhaps in management or in some other form of direct, person to person, communications. If your vocabulary is higher, you will probably do well in some written or more formal communications.

Sequential reasoning test

You are given a string of shapes. You have to work out which two shapes are missing from the string. The missing shapes have been replaced with a 1 and a 2. Choose the correct answers from the possible answers provided on the page. Write in the correct letter that goes with the missing shape. There is space to write in your answers on the right of the page.

Possible answers:

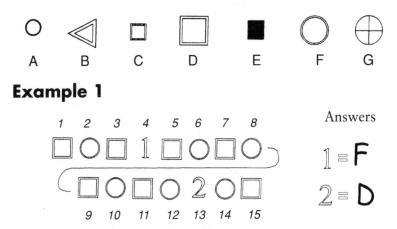

Example 1

Example 2

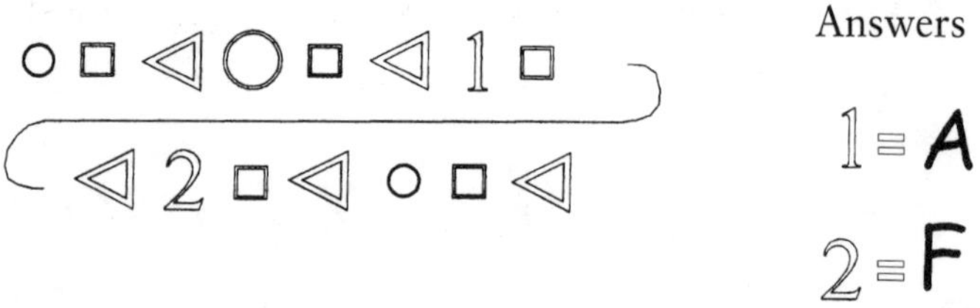

Answers

$1 \equiv$ **A**

$2 \equiv$ **F**

In Example 1, there is a sequence of alternate squares and circles. The fourth in the sequence is a missing circle, so F is correct from the possible answers. Number 13 in the sequence, where a 2 has been placed, should have a square, so D has been written in as the correct answer.

In Example 2, the sequence is triangle, circle, square. A small, white circle would go where the 1 has been placed, so A has been written in. In the sequence, the circles are alternately small and large. A large circle would go where the 2 has been placed, so F has been written in.

The real test is done in just this way. Find the correct answer from those given on each page and write in the letter in the space provided for answers. Both parts must be correct to score.

You have 15 minutes to do as many as you can.

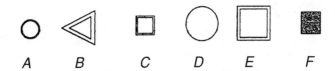

1.

1 2 3 4 5 6 7 8

□ ○ 1 ○ □ ○ □ 2

□ ○ □ ○ □ ○ □

9 10 11 12 13 14 15

1 =
2 =

2.

◁ ○ □ ◁ ○ □ ◁ ○

1 ◁ ○ □ ◁ 2 □

1 =
2 =

3.

□ ○ □ □ ○ □ □ 1

□ □ ○ □ □ ○ 2 □

1 =
2 =

4.

□ ○ ■ □ ○ ■ 1 ○

■ □ ○ 2 □ ○ ■

1 =
2 =

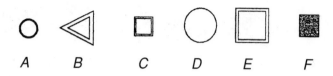

5.

◁ ○ □ ◁ ○ □ ◁ 1)   1 =

(□ ◁ ○ □ ◁ ○ 2   2 =

6.

□ ○ ■ 1 ○ ■ □ ○)   1 =

(■ □ ○ 2 □ ○ ■   2 =

7.

□ ○ □ □ ○ □ 1 ○)   1 =

(□ 2 ○ □ □ ○ □   2 =

8.

1 ○ ■ ○ ○ ■ ○ ○)   1 =

(■ 2 ○ ■ ○   2 =

A   B   C   D   E   F   G   H   I

9.

$1 =$

$2 =$

10.

$1 =$

$2 =$

11.

$1 =$

$2 =$

12.

$1 =$

$2 =$

A   B   C   D   E   F   G   H   I   J   K   L

13.

▪ 1 ☐ ▪ ▪ ☐ ☐ 2

▪ ☐ ☐ ▪

1 =
2 =

14.

△ ○ ▪ 1 △ ○ ▪

▪ 2 ○ ▪

1 =
2 =

15.

△ ▪ 1 ○ 2 ▪ ●

○ △ ■ ● ○ △

1 =
2 =

16.

1 ■ ○ △ ○ 2 ○

△ ○ ■ ○ △ ○ ☐

1 =
2 =

A   B   C   D   E   F   G   H   I   J   K   L

17.

■ ○ □ ■ □ ○ 1 □ ⌐
⌐ □ 2 □ □ ■

1 =
2 =

18.

△ ■ ○ △ △ ■ 1 ⌐
⌐ △ 2 ■ ○ △

1 =
2 =

19.

■ △ 1 ○ ■ △ □ ○ ⌐
⌐ ■ △ □ ○ 2 △

1 =
2 =

20.

○ △ ■ 1 ○ △ □ ● ⌐
⌐ 2 △ □ ○ ● △

1 =
2 =

A B C D E F G H I J K L M N O P Q R

21.

△ ○ 1 ■ △ ○ ▢ □ ⌐
   ▲ 2 ▢ □ △

1 =
2 =

22.

1 △ ■ ○ △ △ ■ ○ ⌐
   △ △ ■ 2 △

1 =
2 =

23.

▲ ▢ ○ △ 1 ▢ ○ ⌐
   △ ▲ ▢ ○ 2 ▲ ▢

1 =
2 =

24.

○ ⊕ ■ ▲ ○ ○ ⊞ ▲ ⌐
   ● 1 ▢ 2 ● ● ▢ △

1 =
2 =

A B C D E F G H I J K L M N O P Q R

25.

○ △ ■ ⊿ ○ △ 1

▲ 2 △ □ △

1 =

2 =

26.

○ ■ ▪ ○ ○ 1 ■

○ ○ ■ 2 ○ ○

1 =

2 =

27.

1 □ ○ ■ ▲ □ ○

□ △ □ ● ■ △ 2

1 =

2 =

28.

⊕ □ ● ▪ △ ⊕ □

● ▪ △ ⊕ 1 2

1 =

2 =

A B C D E F G H I J K L M N O P Q R

29.

■ △ ○ ○ ⊿ □ ▲ 1 ⌇
○ △ ⊞ △ 2 ○ △

1 =
2 =

30.

△ 1 ▪ ○ ⊕ △ ■ ■ ⌇
○ ⊕ △ ▪ ■ ○ 2

1 =
2 =

31.

1 ● □ ○ ⊞ △ ○ □ ● ⌇
□ △ ⊕ 2 ○ □ ▲ ○

1 =
2 =

32.

1 △ ● ⊕ ▪ △ ● ⌇
⊕ ■ △ ● ⊕ 2

1 =
2 =

Answers to sequential reasoning test

1 1=E 2=D	9 1=B 2=G	17 1=B 2=J	25 1=F 2=M
2 1=C 2=D	10 1=F 2=G	18 1=G 2=A	26 1=I 2=B
3 1=A 2=C	11 1=B 2=D	19 1=F 2=B	27 1=E 2=H
4 1=C 2=F	12 1=A 2=I	20 1=G 2=G	28 1=F 2=J
5 1=D 2=E	13 1=H 2=I	21 1=H 2=C	29 1=C 2=J
6 1=E 2=F	14 1=I 2=A	22 1=A 2=C	30 1=B 2=M
7 1=C 2=E	15 1=D 2=E	23 1=K 2=A	31 1=E 2=F
8 1=A 2=A	16 1=G 2=H	24 1=G 2=O	32 1=I 2=I

Obtaining the total score

	number correct =	_____	
	plus 3 if no mistakes	+3 _____	
	Total score =	_____	

Establishing level of potential

below average	average	above average	well above average	exceptional
1–3	4–8	9–12	13–18	19+

Interpretation

In this test a number of sequences thread through each other. It is a complex matter to be able to detect each thread and see how they overlap in order to detect the missing components. In the sense that it contains only visual information, the sequential reasoning test seems to be similar to the perceptual test. However, the way of reasoning in this test is qualitatively different.

The purpose the sequential reasoning test serves is as a further check on your underlying potential. Although most people find this test very demanding indeed, if not downright difficult, it can often show potential that does not appear on the visual, numerical or verbal reasoning tests. In other words, if you obtain a higher score on the sequential reasoning test than on the other reasoning tests, you can be sure that you have potential that you have not used so far.

Often, people with this type of result turn out to be much more successful in their careers than their merely academic results might have predicted. If your score is well above average, compared with your other reasoning scores, you will probably find yourself eventually in a career where you work at the same level or above the level of many graduates or professional people, even though you have no qualifications to speak of yourself. You will probably 'work your way up' in your career, getting promoted because you prove you have initiative and capability, rather than because you have passed examinations that have tested formal skills. You can think quickly and are probably most effective in dealing with practical situations involving people.

Where potential seen on the sequential reasoning test is accompanied by high scores on the other reasoning tests, this would indicate strong and broad abilities that would probably be expressed in high attainments at school and college, and success in a career involving management.

Spatial recognition test

This test explores how easily you can 'see' and turn around objects in space.

You will be shown a shape in the middle of the page. Below it are five other shapes. Each of these is numbered. You have to decide whether each of the alternatives is identical to the original shape. A shape will be the same as the original if it has been turned over or around. It will not be the same as the original if the proportions or parts have been changed. You are to answer each question with a 'Y' for Yes and 'N' for No.

Remember, shapes that are identical to the original, but have been turned around or have been turned over, are marked 'Y'. If it is not either the same or a 'mirror image' you mark 'N'. Try to 'see' the result in your mind.

Example

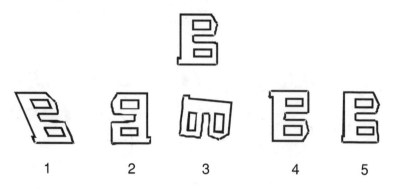

(Answers to example items: 1 N 2 N 3 Y 4 Y 5 N)

You have to work as quickly and as accurately as you can. You have 10 minutes. Start as soon as you are ready.

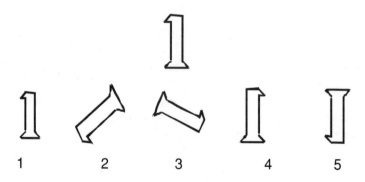

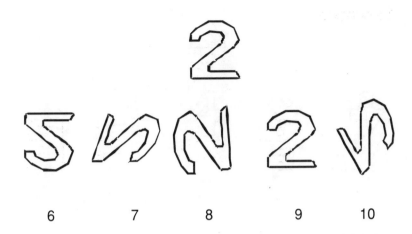

6   7   8   9   10

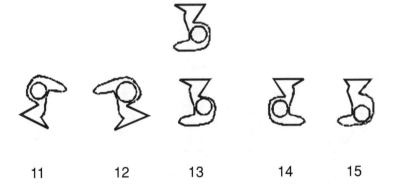

11   12   13   14   15

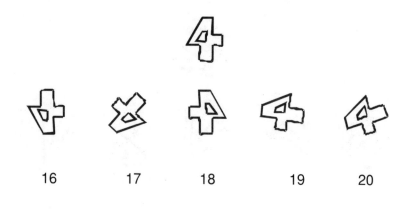

16   17   18   19   20

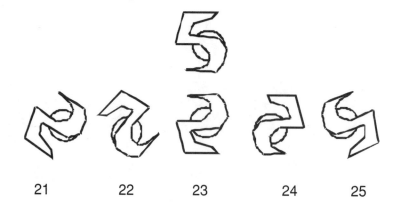

21   22   23   24   25

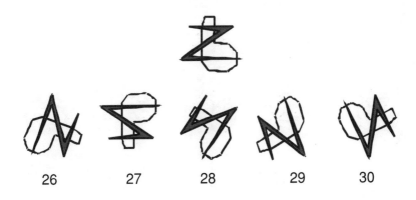

26   27   28   29   30

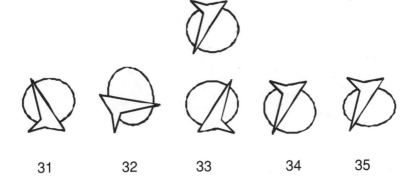

31   32   33   34   35

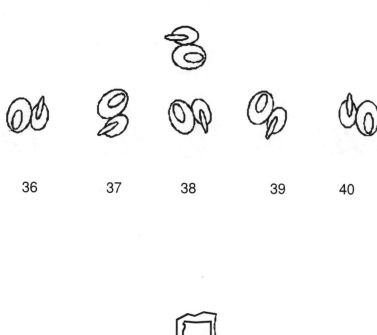

36   37   38   39   40

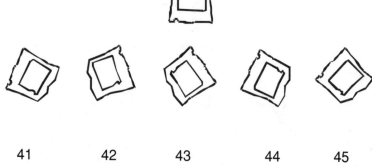

41   42   43   44   45

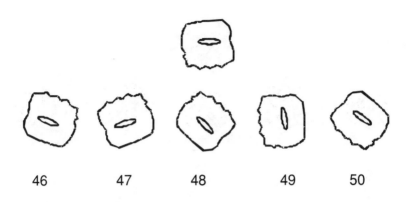

46   47   48   49   50

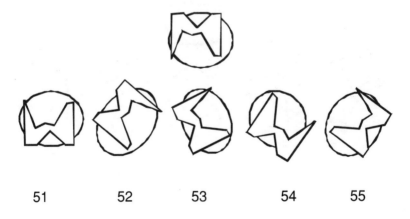

51   52   53   54   55

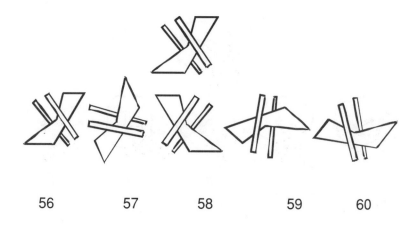

56   57   58   59   60

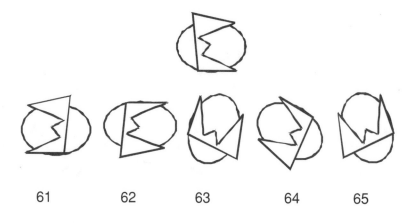

61   62   63   64   65

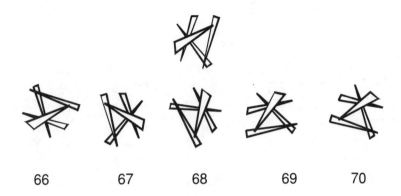

66   67   68   69   70

Answers to spatial recognition test

1 – N	15 – N	29 – N	43 – Y	57 – Y
2 – N	16 – N	30 – Y	44 – Y	58 – Y
3 – Y	17 – Y	31 – N	45 – N	59 – N
4 – Y	18 – Y	32 – N	46 – N	60 – N
5 – Y	19 – Y	33 – Y	47 – Y	61 – N
6 – Y	20 – Y	34 – N	48 – N	62 – N
7 – N	21 – Y	35 – N	49 – Y	63 – Y
8 – N	22 – Y	36 – Y	50 – N	64 – Y
9 – Y	23 – N	37 – N	51 – N	65 – Y
10 – N	24 – N	38 – N	52 – N	66 – Y
11 – Y	25 – Y	39 – Y	53 – N	67 – N
12 – N	26 – N	40 – Y	54 – N	68 – Y
13 – N	27 – Y	41 – N	55 – Y	69 – Y
14 – Y	28 – N	42 – N	56 – N	70 – N

Obtaining the total score

	number correct =	_____	
	take away half the number of errors	– _____	
	Total score =	_____	

Establishing level of potential

below average	average	above average	well above average	exceptional
1–9	10–26	27–34	35–42	43+

Interpretation

A similar test, with different items, was also given in my book *Career, Aptitude & Selection Tests*. It is a useful test because it often detects raw, natural potential to perceive abstract problems as well as those that often relate to art and design.

The ability to cope with rotating shapes is in some way the equivalent of 'turning things over in the mind' – an ability that is relevant to many areas of endeavour where flexibility of thinking is important. Often, people who do well on this test are seen as original or imaginative because they seem to create new possibilities or outcomes. If you can do well on this test you may well be perceived as someone who comes up with ideas that are new or different.

How this potential expresses itself is usually determined by how it combines with other areas of potential. It may reveal a purely artistic potential, but could also appear in subjects such as computing and systems, technology, and geography. If accompanied by verbal ability, you may well be drawn to careers where you can be involved with ideas and cultural activities, such as writing or media work.

Three-D test

In this test you are asked to discover the hidden sides of objects. You are shown a stack of blocks. Each block is exactly the same size. You can see the front, or facing, sides. You can also see the top side. But you cannot see the two sides that are hidden from your view. Nor can you see the bottom, or underneath, side. However, you can imagine what the hidden sides and underneath must look like.

In the example on the next page, there is a stack of five blocks. You have to imagine, out of the five possibilities you are given, which one is the view from side A. Only one of the five is correct. Then, do the same for sides B and C. In each set of possibilities, only one is correct, even though it may have been turned around. Tick the correct one.

Example

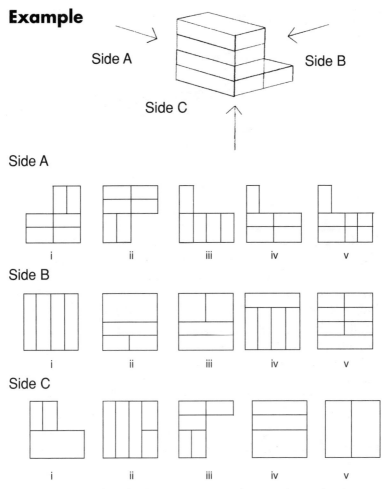

Side A

Side B

Side C

For the example, the answer is number iii for side A, even though it has been turned around. For side B, number i is the correct answer. Number v is the correct answer for side C.

You may find it helpful to have spare paper available. For each example, tick the correct choice out of the five options given for each side. Be careful, as the view may have been turned around. You have five minutes to do as many as you can.

1.

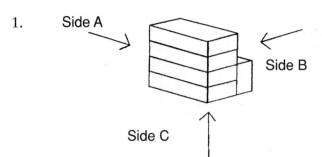

Side A

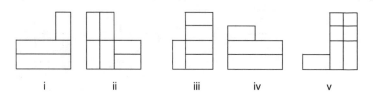

i	ii	iii	iv	v

Side B

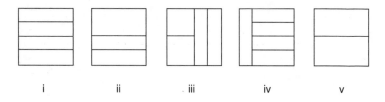

i	ii	iii	iv	v

Side C

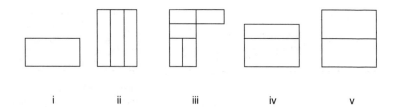

i	ii	iii	iv	v

2.

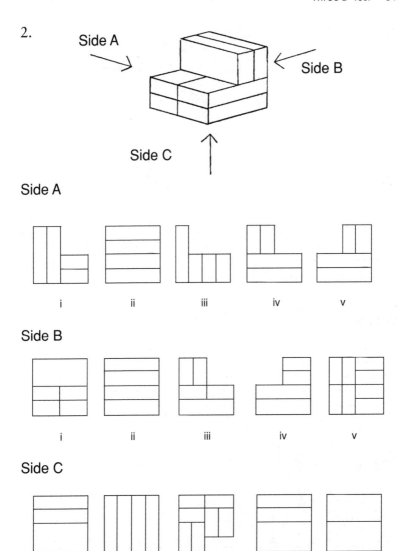

Side A

| i | ii | iii | iv | v |

Side B

| i | ii | iii | iv | v |

Side C

| i | ii | iii | iv | v |

3.

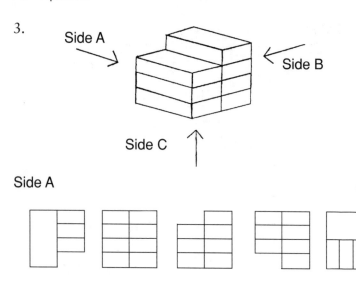

Side A

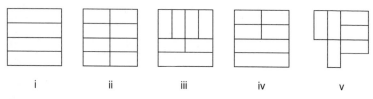

| i | ii | iii | iv | v |

Side B

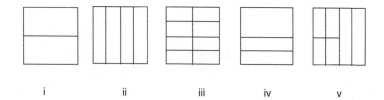

| i | ii | iii | iv | v |

Side C

| i | ii | iii | iv | v |

4.

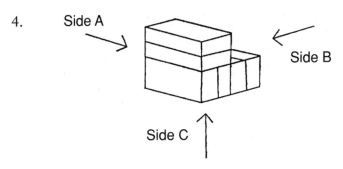

Side A

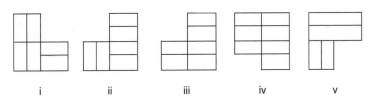

i   ii   iii   iv   v

Side B

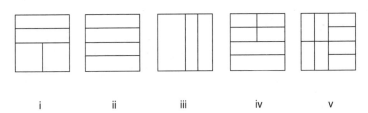

i   ii   iii   iv   v

Side C

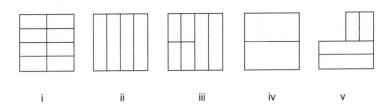

i   ii   iii   iv   v

5.

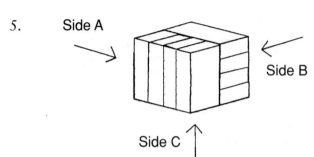

Side A

| i | ii | iii | iv | v |

Side B

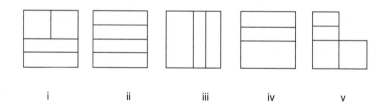

| i | ii | iii | iv | v |

Side C

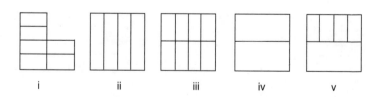

| i | ii | iii | iv | v |

6.

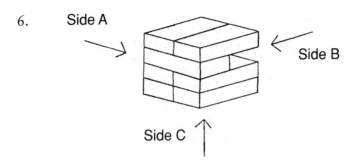

Side A
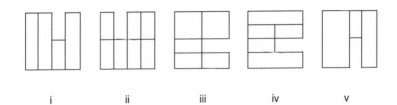

Side B
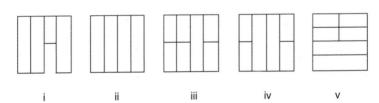

Side C

7.

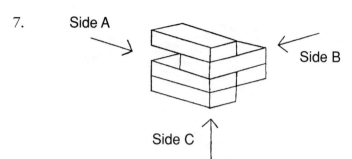

Side A

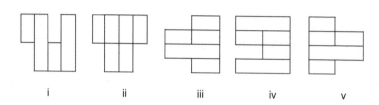

i   ii   iii   iv   v

Side B

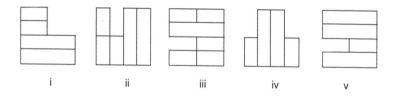

i   ii   iii   iv   v

Side C

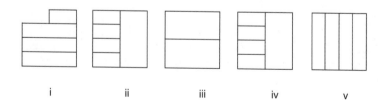

i   ii   iii   iv   v

8.

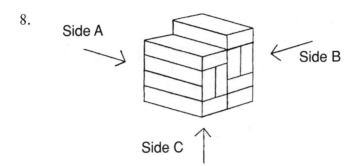

Side A

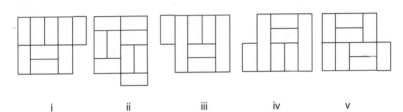

i   ii   iii   iv   v

Side B

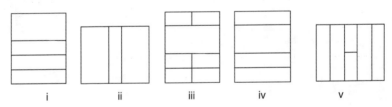

i   ii   iii   iv   v

Side C

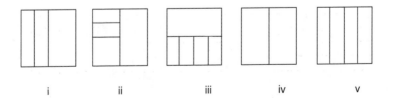

i   ii   iii   iv   v

9.

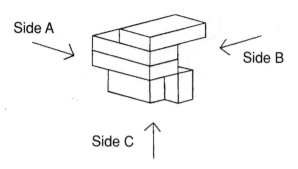

Side A

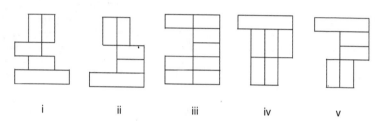

i   ii   iii   iv   v

Side B

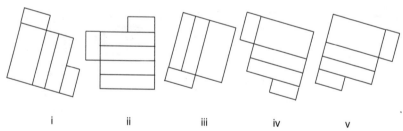

i   ii   iii   iv   v

Side C

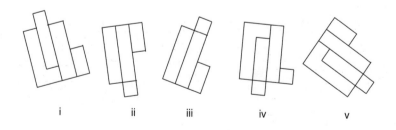

i   ii   iii   iv   v

10.

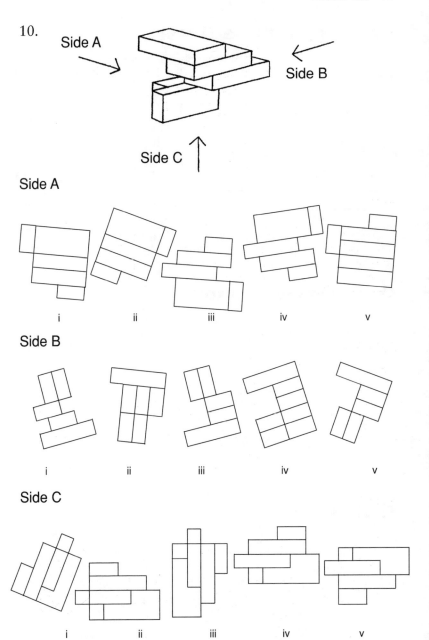

Side A

Side B

Side C

Answers to three-D test

1	A– iii	B – ii	C – iv
2	A – iv	B – ii	C – v
3	A – iv	B – i	C – i
4	A – ii	B – iii	C – ii
5	A – iv	B – ii	C – v
6	A – i	B – iii	C– ii
7	A – v	B – v	C – iii
8	A – ii	B – iv	C– iv
9	A – v	B – iv	C – i
10	A – iii	B – iii	C – v

Obtaining the total score

	number correct =	_____	
	plus 3 if no mistakes	+3 _____	
	Total score =	_____	

Establishing level of potential

below average	average	above average	well above average	exceptional
1–6	7–12	13–16	17–21	22+

Interpretation

This test demands many of the same attributes as the test of spatial recognition. However, it does not distort the shapes in the same way, and the shapes themselves are regular.

Though the three-D is often an indicator of creative potential in the same way as the spatial recognition tests, it is usually predictive of success in areas that are more formal and require a more structured, technical approach, as in architecture and many forms of planning, for example.

This test is also different from the spatial recognition test, because the objects are specifically three-dimensional, not flat. This has implications for the way you think. Psychologically, it requires that you are able to 'look behind what appears on the surface of things'. You have to form a representation in your mind of what is on the other side. Literally, you have to conceive a diagram or picture that exists nowhere but in your own mind, which you infer from the original presented to you.

Possibly because the test demands that you bring an image together in your mind to form a unified whole, it was once thought that this type of test was the purest measure of intelligence. There is no doubt that it is another good measure of hard, natural intelligence. It will come to the surface in some way, even though it is not accompanied by the more formal verbal, numerical or visual aptitudes. People who have this type of potential are almost always recognized as intelligent, even though they may not necessarily do as well as expected in educational settings; they often do better when they have left formal schooling.

However, this aptitude by itself may express itself in design, drawing and craft skills. With numerical reasoning it would suggest professional training in areas connected with engineering and technology.

Systems test

In this test you are given a series of letters and symbols at the top of each page. Each letter goes with a particular symbol. The letter is in the top box of each pair and the symbol is at the bottom.

Your task is to write in the letter that goes with each symbol. The example below shows you how. The first nine have been done already. Complete the last three yourself.

Example

A	B	C	D	E	F	G	H	I	J	K	L
✈	⊕	☞	🕯	❄	✡	✝	✋	卍	💣	☯	☪

Example answer

1	2	3	4	5	6	7	8	9	10	11	12
D	G	J	H	D	F	A	K	C			
🕯	✝	💣	✋	🕯	✡	✈	☯	☞	🕯	✈	⊕

The answers to 10, 11 and 12 are D, A and B.

On each page, look at the symbols that go with each letter at the top of the page. Then write in the missing letter that goes with each symbol for each of the test items. It is important to go as quickly as possible without making mistakes. You have exactly four minutes and you must get as many correct as possible in the time allowed.

A	B	C	D	E	F	G	H	I	J	K	L

1	2	3	4	5	6	7	8	9	10	11	12

13	14	15	16	17	18	19	20	21	22	23	24

25	26	27	28	29	30	31	32	33	34	35	36

37	38	39	40	41	42	43	44	45	46	47	48

49	50	51	52	53	54	55	56	57	58	59	60

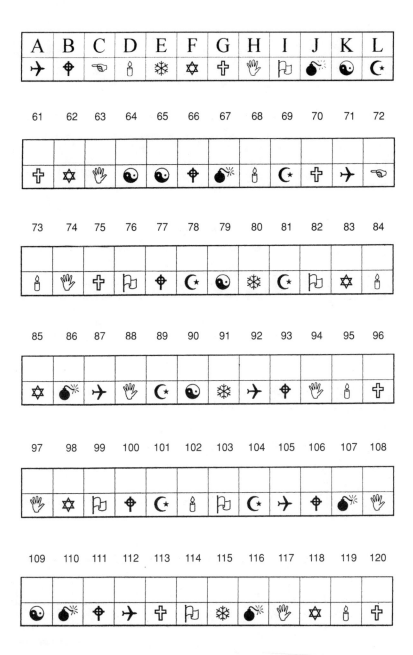

A	B	C	D	E	F	G	H	I	J	K	L
✈	☥	☞	🕯	❄	✡	✝	✋	🚩	💣	☯	☪

M	N	O	P	Q	R	S	T	U	V	W	X
❖	♌	■	●	&	♒	♎	♋	📫	♓	⌂	◆

121	122	123	124	125	126	127	128	129	130	131	132
✋	🚩	💣	☯	☪	♋	📫	♓	◆	✈	☥	

133	134	135	136	137	138	139	140	141	142	143	144
&	✡	✝	■	✋	🚩	💣	☯	☪	♌	✝	♒

145	146	147	148	149	150	151	152	153	154	155	156
♌	♒	✈	✈	☥	📫	&	☞	❖	◆	■	💣

157	158	159	160	161	162	163	164	165	166	167	168
♌	♒	✈	✈	☥	📫	&	☞	❖	◆	■	💣

A	B	C	D	E	F	G	H	I	J	K	L
✈	⊕	☞	🕯	❄	✡	✝	✋	⚑	💣	☯	☾★

M	N	O	P	Q	R	S	T	U	V	W	X
❖	♌	■	●	&	≈≈	♎	♋	✉	♓	◫	◆

169	170	171	172	173	174	175	176	177	178	179	180
&	☾★	≈≈	✉	♌	&	■	⚑	💣	✡	✋	♎

181	182	183	184	185	186	187	188	189	190	191	192
◆	✡	✝	✋	■	✈	☾★	🕯	❄	&	❖	☞

193	194	195	196	197	198	199	200	201	202	203	204
✉	♌	♎	☞	❖	☾★	◆	≈≈	✋	⚑	💣	■

205	206	207	208	209	210	211	212	213	214	215	216
◆	❖	☞	✉	♎	✈	☞	🕯	☾★	🕯	❄	≈≈

Answers to systems test

It is rare for people to make more than the odd or occasional mistake on this test. You can check, if you wish, for absolute accuracy, but the number of items you have attempted is likely to provide a reliable overall answer. If, however, you think you may have been guessing, and have therefore probably made some mistakes, you should go back and check what you have done, and take the number of errors you have made away from the number attempted.

Obtaining the total score

	number correct =		
		_____	

Establishing level of potential

below average	average	above average	well above average	exceptional
1–30	31–100	101–132	133–165	166+

Interpretation

This is a demanding test because it can become tedious while at the same time demanding absolute concentration.

The way you attempted the test can be revealing. Most people check off symbols one by one as they appear. A variant of this approach is to take one symbol at a time, checking off all the same symbols on the page. If you have approached the test in one of these ways you are measuring your aptitude for checking and organization.

Another method is more conceptual, involving memorizing each one of the items as they become familiar. In this process the letter becomes identified with the symbol and takes its place. People who use this method eventually are quick on this test because they eliminate the time required for checking. If you made use of this method you are also measuring your aptitude for the memorization and recognition of information.

This aptitude is essential where attention to detail is required, as in many administrative situations. However, people who use the 'memory approach' may be at a disadvantage if they are presented with constantly new information to check, because this gives them no opportunity to form a concept they can retain in their memory to help them. They come into their own in dealing with information where they are expected to impose some sort of system or conceptual framework upon the information. In other words, they may be more adept at sorting out problems of order rather than checking the correctness of items.

Precision is usually appreciated in careers involving financial transactions and in legal work. The same type of ability is demanded in computer programming and analysis.

8

Vocabulary test

This is a test of your understanding of words. You are given a word and have to say which one of the alternatives is closest in meaning to it. You have to place a tick in the correct box. Look at the examples below.

Examples

1. OWN		2. ADD	
☑	a) possess	☐	a) subtract
☐	b) unpaid	☑	b) count
☐	c) disown	☐	c) duke
☐	d) landlord	☐	d) new

In Example 1, to *possess* means the same as to *own*. If you think of a sentence with the word *own* in it, you will find that the word *possess* could replace it. For example, 'I *own* a car – I *possess* a car.' *Unpaid* means owing, not to *own*. *Disown* means the opposite of to own. *Landlord* means an owner, not to *own*. *Own* and *possess* are verbs, while *unpaid* is an adjective, *disown* is a verb, but means the opposite of *own*; and *landlord* is a noun.

In Example 2, *subtract* is the opposite of *add*, although it is a verb, as *add* is a verb. *Duke* is a noun, but does not mean *add*. *New* means fresh, and therefore could be added, but it would not be able to replace the *word* add in a sentence. In any case, fresh is an adjective. Both *add* and *count* are verbs. *Count* is the answer, because it is almost identical in meaning to add and could easily replace it in a sentence, for example, 'You should ADD up your money – You should count up your money.' It does not matter that *count* can have other meanings, for example, as a noun in 'The Count and Countess were invited to the palace.'

You can have as much time as you want to do this test, but it is probably not worth spending any longer than five minutes, as you will find that you either know the meanings of the words, or you do not.

Place a tick in the box of the alternative that is closest in meaning to the word in capitals.

1. BAD	2. WET
☐ a) evil	☐ a) appetite
☐ b) angel	☐ b) strong
☐ c) good	☐ c) watery
☐ d) ban	☐ d) dry

3. CHIEF	4. CHOP
☐ a) mainly	☐ a) rough
☐ b) minor	☐ b) duty
☐ c) head	☐ c) stormy
☐ d) unimportant	☐ d) divide

5. SOFT	6. GOWN
☐ a) harsh	☐ a) sack
☐ b) undemanding	☐ b) shout
☐ c) contact	☐ c) robe
☐ d) comfort	☐ d) about

7. IMAGINARY	8. ACTIVE
☐ a) realistic	☐ a) mobile
☐ b) bleak	☐ b) baffle
☐ c) trance	☐ c) rigid
☐ d) dreamy	☐ d) motion

9. PIERCE	10. INVALUABLE
☐ a) puncture	☐ a) worthless
☐ b) stung	☐ b) valuable
☐ c) loud	☐ c) variable
☐ d) stabbing	☐ d) cheap

11. ADAPT	12. IMPARTIAL
☐ a) convert	☐ a) connected
☐ b) flexible	☐ b) detached
☐ c) inflexible	☐ c) involved
☐ d) transformation	☐ d) unconcern

13. REPUTABLE

- ☐ a) infamous
- ☐ b) supposed
- ☐ c) good
- ☐ d) stature

14. LIGHTEN

- ☐ a) discover
- ☐ b) darken
- ☐ c) illumine
- ☐ d) weak

15. GROUNDLESS

- ☐ a) justified
- ☐ b) background
- ☐ c) basis
- ☐ d) absurd

16. FASTEN

- ☐ a) affix
- ☐ b) untie
- ☐ c) holder
- ☐ d) thin

17. BARGAINING

- ☐ a) trafficking
- ☐ b) anticipate
- ☐ c) promise
- ☐ d) agree

18. WORRISOME

- ☐ a) reassuring
- ☐ b) unworried
- ☐ c) annoy
- ☐ d) perturbing

19. UNDERCURRENT

- ☐ a) undercharge
- ☐ b) atmosphere
- ☐ c) undermine
- ☐ d) belittle

20. SATANIC

- ☐ a) divine
- ☐ b) devil
- ☐ c) inhuman
- ☐ d) biting

21. PRICELESS	22. MUTINOUS
☐ a) prized	☐ a) defiance
☐ b) cheap	☐ b) uprising
☐ c) menu	☐ c) obedient
☐ d) expense	☐ d) turbulent

23. HOMELY	24. FUNCTIONAL
☐ a) mother	☐ a) plain
☐ b) domestic	☐ b) official
☐ c) formal	☐ c) decorative
☐ d) revered	☐ d) gathering

25. EXEMPT	26. GALLANT
☐ a) spared	☐ a) cowardly
☐ b) liable	☐ b) escort
☐ c) except	☐ c) courageousness
☐ d) illustrate	☐ d) polite

27. EXPRESSLY	28. DAPPER
☐ a) assert	☐ a) sloppy
☐ b) energetic	☐ b) spry
☐ c) particularly	☐ c) bespeckled
☐ d) vaguely	☐ d) dappled

29. COGNIZANT

- ☐ a) unaware
- ☐ b) apprehension
- ☐ c) acquainted
- ☐ d) perception

30. PORTEND

- ☐ a) presage
- ☐ b) insignificant
- ☐ c) presentiment
- ☐ d) emblazon

31. BENEDICTION

- ☐ a) anathema
- ☐ b) benevolence
- ☐ c) munificence
- ☐ d) blessing

32. CONCOMITANT

- ☐ a) coincidental
- ☐ b) accidental
- ☐ c) incidental
- ☐ d) compressed

33. GUILELESS

- ☐ a) artful
- ☐ b) shame
- ☐ c) innocent
- ☐ d) transparent

34. CULMINATE

- ☐ a) crown
- ☐ b) peak
- ☐ c) begin
- ☐ d) pursue

35. EXONERATE

- ☐ a) absolution
- ☐ b) inflate
- ☐ c) incriminate
- ☐ d) vindicate

36. ICONOCLASTIC

- ☐ a) denunciatory
- ☐ b) credulity
- ☐ c) uncritical
- ☐ d) optimistic

37. IMPLICIT	38. PENURIOUS
☐ a) innuendo	☐ a) paucity
☐ b) explicit	☐ b) indigent
☐ c) latent	☐ c) dearth
☐ d) stated	☐ d) meditative

39. SPURIOUS	40. TRANSMOGRIFY
☐ a) authentic	☐ a) attitudinize
☐ b) specious	☐ b) traverse
☐ c) sordid	☐ c) mutation
☐ d) dishevelled	☐ d) metamorphose

Answers to vocabulary test

1 – a	9 – a	17 – a	25 – a	33 – c
2 – c	10 – b	18 – d	26 – d	34 – b
3 – c	11 – a	19 – b	27 – c	35 – d
4 – d	12 – b	20 – c	28 – b	36 – a
5 – b	13 – c	21 – a	29 – c	37 – c
6 – c	14 – c	22 – d	30 – a	38 – b
7 – d	15 – d	23 – b	31 – d	39 – b
8 – a	16 – a	24 – a	32 – c	40 – d

Obtaining the total score

	number correct =	_____
plus 4 if you are aged under 16	plus 2 if aged 17–20	+ _____
	Total score =	_____

Establishing level of potential

below average	average	above average	well above average	exceptional
1–6	7–19	20–25	26–30	31+

Interpretation

The vocabulary test may be regarded as a test of knowledge like any learnt skill, and therefore different from most of the other tests, which look at more abstract, underlying potential. It is true that the vocabulary is not measuring innate intelligence, that is, what you were born with. However, it is measuring a means by which intelligence is choosing to express itself. Through the use of words, bearing in mind that words form concepts, there is scope for clear analysis and expression of information as well as abstract ideas. It is certainly an area of potential that is relevant to career success.

Lack of a strong vocabulary will probably not hold you back in your career, provided you have other areas of potential that are more important for the task or type of work on which you are engaged. It will obviously hold you back in areas of communication in which a high vocabulary is expected. Typically, students on technically oriented courses do less well on vocabulary tests than those who are pursuing arts courses such as English, history, languages or philosophy. All these demand that words be used correctly and precisely.

Although a comparatively strong vocabulary may not necessarily be essential to success, many people gain promotion to a level where they believe that lack of vocabulary is a serious disadvantage. If your vocabulary is lower than your other test scores, you can certainly take it that you have the potential to improve your vocabulary.

9

Figurework test

In this test you are asked to work out various sums and calculations. The test involves arithmetic and will test you on decimals, percentages and fractions. You are not allowed a calculator on this test.

In this test: '+' means add, '−' means take away or subtract, 'X' means multiply or times, '/' means divide by.

For each problem write in the correct answer in the space provided on the right-hand side. Look at the examples below. The first one has been done for you.

Answer

Example 1

10/2 = ? 5

_____

Example 2

What is 50% of £20? _____

Example 3

What is 3 X ½?   _____

Example 4

1.3 – (minus) 0.9 = ?   _____

In Example 2, the answer is £10. 50% is the same as 50 parts out of 100 or the same as 5 parts in 10. One part in 10 of £20 is £2, so 5 parts is £10.

In Example 3 the answer is 1½. Three half-parts makes one and a half parts, which is the same as half of three.

In Example 4 the answer is 0.4. This is 13 parts take away 9 parts and then putting back the decimal point in the correct place.

Make sure you have scrap paper for any rough working you may want do on this test. Please do not mark the book if it is not your own. You have 10 minutes for this test. Work as quickly and as accurately as you can. Begin as soon as you are ready.

Answer

1. 10 – 5 = ?   _____

2. What is 10% of £40?   _____

3. What is 4 X ½ (half of 4)?   _____

4. 1.6 – (minus) 0.3 = ?   _____

5. 21/7 = ?   _____

6. What is 5% of £40?   _____

7. What is 8 X ¼?   _____

8. 2.1 + 1.9 = ?   _____

9. 10 X 13 = ?   _____

10. What is 3% of £100?   _____

11. What is 16 X ¼?   _____

12. 3.08 + 2.19 = ?   _____

13. 156 / 12 = ?   _____

14. What is 1/3 X 1/3 ?   _____

15. What is 7½% of £300?   _____

16. What is 15 / 2½?   _____

17. 106.7 – 103.81 = ?   _____

18. What is 32/50 as a percentage?   _____

19. A rectangular floor measures   _____
    2.5 metres by 3 metres. What
    is the size of the floor in square
    metres?

20. What is 22½% of £200?   _____

21. What is 4 ¼ X ¼?   _____

22. 0.07 X 0.02 = ?   _____

23. 17 X 29 = ?   _____

24. What is 6% of £40 added   _____
     to 12½% of £20?

25. What is 6 divided by 8?   _____

26. Divide 0.09 by 0.3   _____

27. From £50 how much change   _____
     will you have if you purchase as
     many items as possible
     each costing £1.99?

28. How many dollars will I get   _____
     for £10 if the exchange rate is
     1.45 dollars to the pound?

29. The interest on a £1000 loan   _____
     is 20% annually. What is the
     total amount of interest paid
     at the end of year two?

30. If an item cost £126 when   _____
     discounted to 60% of its
     original price what was
     the original price?

Answers to figurework test

1 – 5	9 – 130	17 – 2.89	25 – 0.75 or 3/4
2 – £4	10 – £3	18 – 64%	26 – 0.3
3 – 2	11 – 4	19 – 7.5	27 – 25p
4 – 1.3	12 – 5.27	20 – £45	28 – £14.50
5 – 3	13 – 13	21 – 1 1/16	29 – £440
6 – £2	14 – 1/9	22 – 0.0014	30 – £210
7 – 2	15 – £22.50	23 – 493	
8 – 4	16 – 6	24 – £4.90	

Obtaining the total score

	number correct =	_____
plus 2 if aged under 15	plus 1 if aged 16–18	+ _____
	Total score =	_____

Establishing level of potential

below average	average	above average	well above average	exceptional
1–3	4–6	7–12	13–18	19+

Interpretation

The figurework test is assessing your skills in everyday situations where arithmetic is essential. All of us do figurework all the time in relation to our personal finances and in various practical situations where calculating and estimating are necessary parts of daily life. But some people have a liking for this type of activity or a talent for it that then leads them to think of careers in which they are dealing with money, estimating or performing other arithmetical functions. The range of careers that require these skills is vast and also extremely varied.

There is no doubt that skill in this area can be improved. All of the sums in the test depend upon an understanding of the rules of numbers, and numerical 'fluency' does depend to a large degree upon practice. Many people know their multiplication tables because they chanted them in school so much that they were drummed in. Boring though this might have been, the repetition of the exercises has probably produced a skill that has a lifelong usefulness. Many people will declare that these days they leave such figurework to a calculator or to a computer and therefore they have become rusty. Nevertheless, to do well in this test requires an underlying aptitude, which will appear as an above average score, even though you may not have used the skills you were taught at school for a while.

In many careers, the basic calculation has to be summed up quickly, even if it is a rough approximation, in order that a decision can be reached in principle. This happens in many areas of financial assessment, costing, surveying work as well as in buying and selling. Often, people really are thinking on their feet when they use their figurework skills, and you will know from your own experience that there have been times when you have to think quickly in order not to be caught out.

If you like these kinds of problems and do well on this test you may think of careers as diverse as banking, insurance, costing, purchasing as well as many other forms of quantitative, administrative and commercial work.

10

Aptitude profiling and 'IQ'

Level of score

'Average' means that you scored about as well as most other people on a test. Therefore, no especial aptitude has been detected on this occasion. You may have an aptitude for a type of problem solving that has not been detected by the specific test. It could be that the areas of work that may be predicted by this test may be less suited to you than those suggested by other tests where there is stronger evidence. Areas of work suggested by results providing the strongest evidence are the ones that will most likely be where you will find it easiest to be successful.

On page 105 you will find a chart titled 'Your aptitude profile'. Place your own scores in the chart by circling your own score in the appropriate place.

If you connect up the scores, you should have a graph that looks something like the example:

Example profile

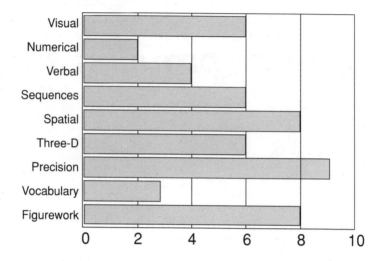

Your aptitude profile

Mark the place where each of your test results falls in the chart. You can draw a bar from the left of the chart to your score, to form a bar line, as in the example profile above.

Test	below average	average	above average	well above average	exceptional
	1 2	3 4	5 6	7 8	9 10
VISUAL	1-2	3-7	8-13	14-20	21+
NUMERICAL	1-2	3-5	6-8	9-13	14+
VERBAL	1-3	4-8	9-12	13-17	18+
SEQUENCES	1-3	4-8	9-12	13-19	20+
SPATIAL	1-9	10-26	27-34	35-42	43+
THREE-D	1-6	7-12	13-16	17-21	22+
SYSTEMS	1-30	31-100	101-132	133-165	166+
VOCABULARY	1-6	7-19	20-25	26-30	31+
FIGUREWORK	1-3	4-6	7-12	13-18	19+

Differences between scores

Your profile readily enables you to see possible differences between your scores. These differences may not be significant. For example, on another occasion, your differences between scores might be reversed, so that on one occasion you seem to do better with verbal than with visual reasoning, but on the next occasion do better with visual reasoning than with verbal reasoning. This may be because you are really equally good on both tests. It may be that tiredness, or other reasons, affect your performance on different occasions.

However, the greater the difference between tests, the more likely it is that you really are better on one type of test than another. This difference may be important to you in determining the most suitable area of study or what career to pursue.

If your test scores are different from what you had assumed and if you disagree with the results there is no reason why you should not place your own estimates of your potential, if these are different from your test results, in the chart. It depends on how far you agree that the test results are fully and accurately assessing you. There is always room for some doubt. As discussed in the Introduction, your results on the tests might be affected by all sorts of issues relating to:

- the efficiency with which you test yourself;
- the conditions in which you test yourself;
- who you compare yourself with;
- whether the tests themselves have reliably detected your potential.

Therefore, your own estimates might be based upon your progress at school and upon other experiences.

As a rough guide, take it that if there is a clear section between two scores, there may be a significant difference in your aptitude. For example, if your score on one test is in the upper section of well above average and another score is in the upper part of above average, there will be a section (clear score area) between the two scores. You can become more certain, the more sections there are between the two scores. To make this clear, each of your scores on the tests will fall under a number 1–10 written under each chart. So, for example, there may not be any real difference between a score of 5 and 6, but there is likely to be a real difference in your potential if the scores are 5 and 7. The greater the difference between scores, the greater the difference between your potential in the two fields. How much weight you place upon the difference between any two scores is, in the end, for you to judge.

Interpretation of your profile is reasonably easy if you have one result which stands out from the others. There remains the difficulty of relating this aptitude to a career: even a distinct aptitude may translate into numerous career options.

Most people will obtain a pattern where there is no single, distinguishable aptitude, but rather a pattern that appears to consist of relative highs and lows. Your highest score might be the best indication, but also look at any other relatively high scores.

Do your scores seem to group themselves in any way? How are your high scores different from your lower scores? What, broadly, do the relative highs and lows tell you? Some people do better with all the word and numerical types of test, but not visual types and spatial types. This would be interpreted as more of an administrative as opposed to an artistic pattern. Others may do well on both the numerical and visual tests, but not so well on the verbal side. This might indicate more of a scientific bias. There are, of course, many possible patterns for you to interpret.

The level of the various scores is not particularly relevant and you may have other high scores besides those that are frequently indicative of potential in certain areas. Your own pattern is most unlikely to be identical to the following common patterns, but you may find them useful for general guidance.

Accountancy and Finance

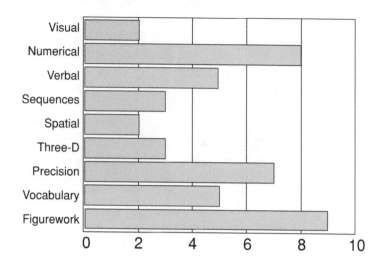

Agriculture and Land Management

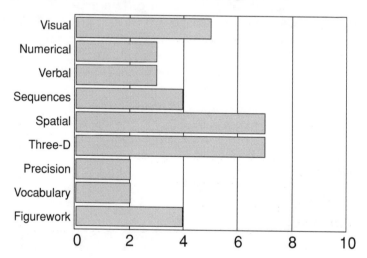

Architecture

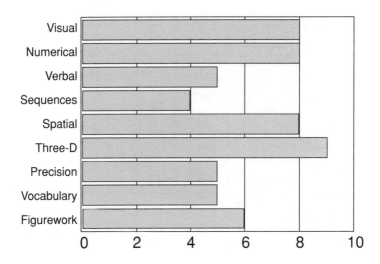

Art and Design

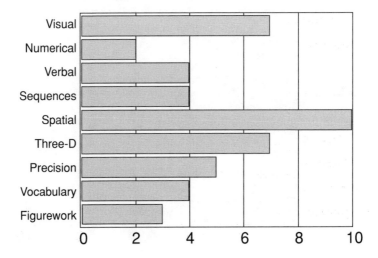

Art History

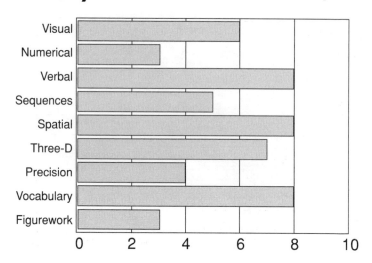

Biology and Biological Sciences

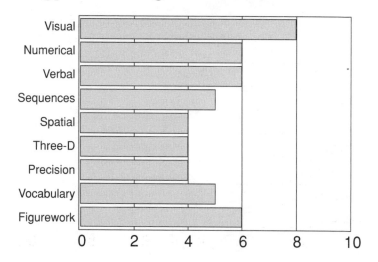

Catering

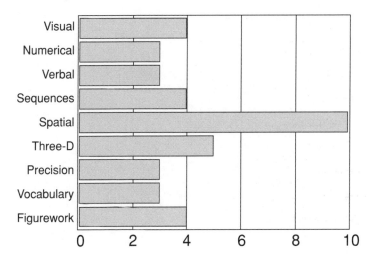

Chemistry

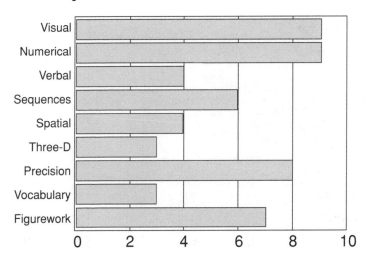

Classics

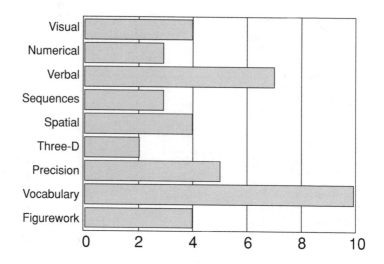

Computing and IT

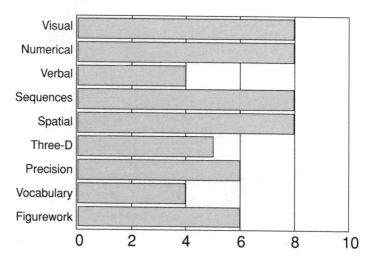

Craft

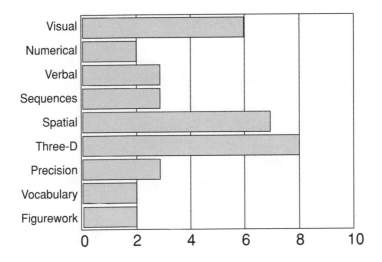

Dance

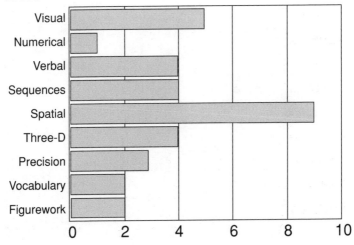

Drama

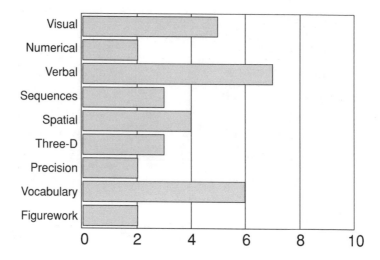

Ecology and Environmental Sciences

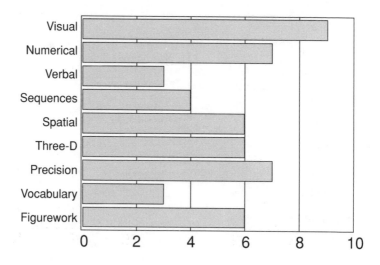

Economics

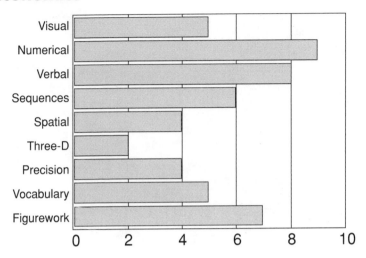

Engineering

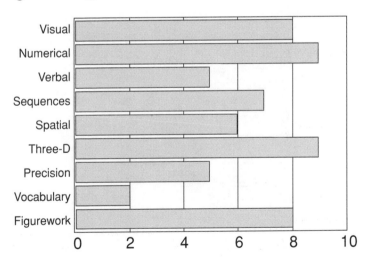

English

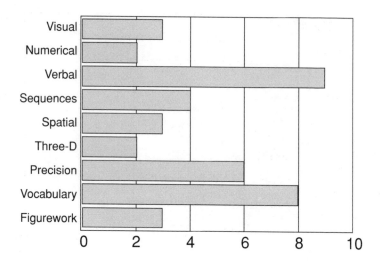

Fashion

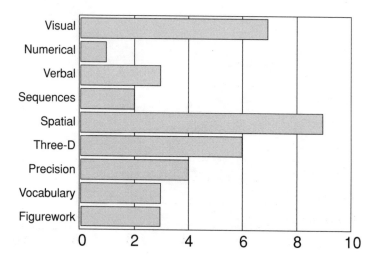

Geography

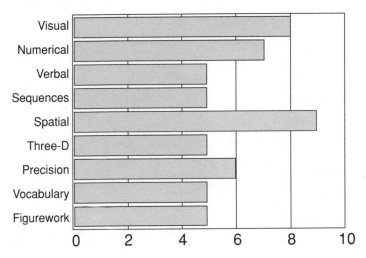

History

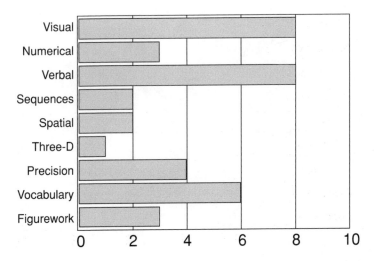

Hotel Management

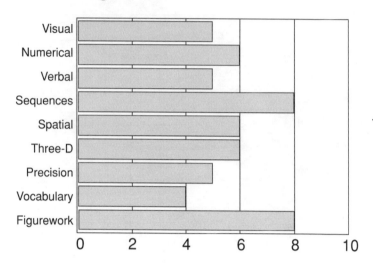

Languages and Linguistics

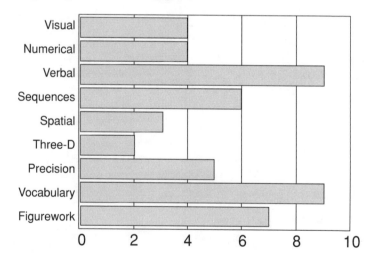

Law

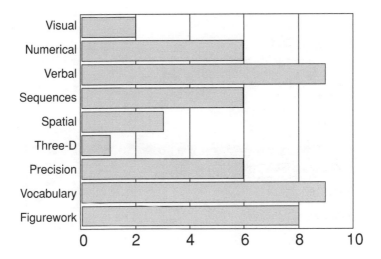

Library and Information Science

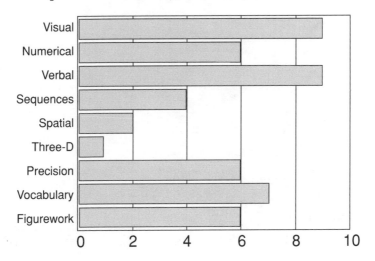

Mathematics and Statistics

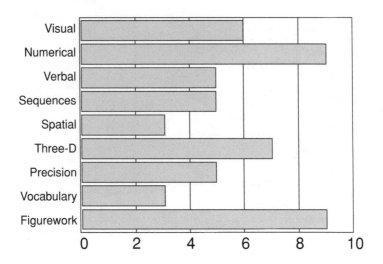

Media and Communication

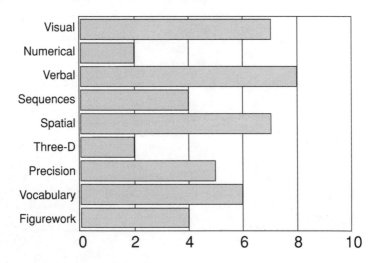

Music

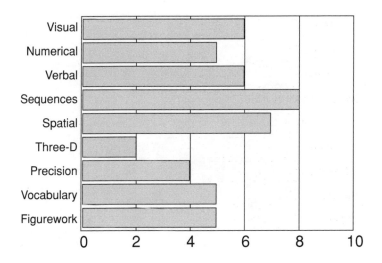

Nursing

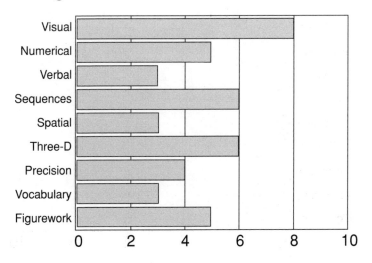

Philosophy and Religious Studies

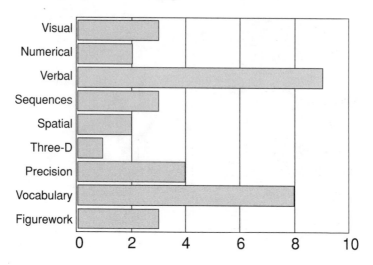

Physics

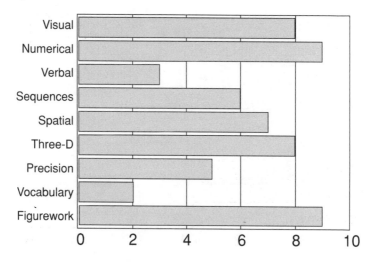

Politics and International Relations

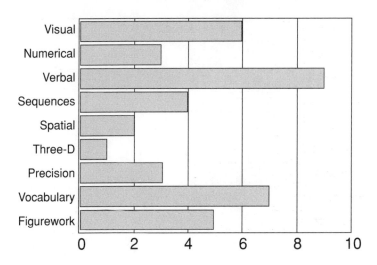

Psychology

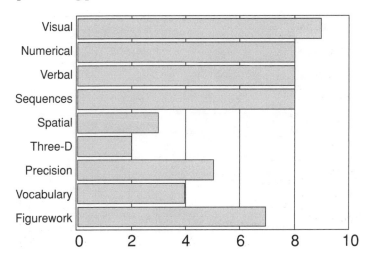

Sociology

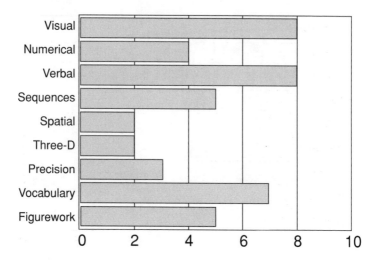

Sport and Leisure Studies

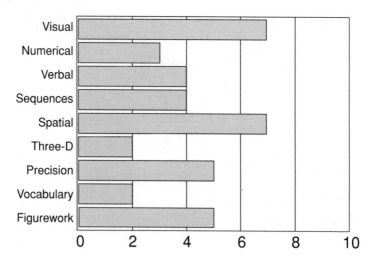

Textile Technology

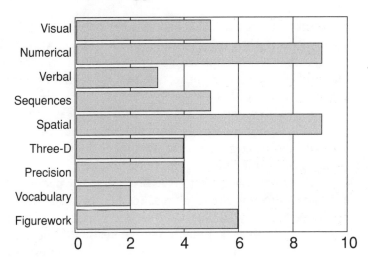

Veterinary Medicine

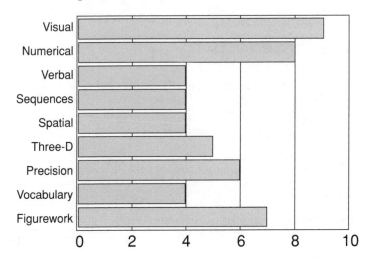

IQ

Your IQ (intelligence quotient) is a number by which you can compare yourself with other people. In an indirect way, you have already been doing this with your test results in this book. All that an IQ does is attempt to give you more precise information as to where you stand on the comparative scale.

This book cannot measure your IQ with any great accuracy, as the conditions for measuring your IQ, as well as the information required to compare your intelligence with a satisfactory sample of people like you, are not available.

Why then, provide a guide to IQ? Because many people find the exercise interesting for its own sake. And because the tests in this book are very similar to other tests used to measure intelligence, it enables a fuller comprehension of the entire process of intellectual measurement. Furthermore, an estimate of IQ provides a quick way of asking yourself whether you are going in a direction with your studies or in your career that will allow you to fully use your potential.

Intelligence tests

These are designed to assess innate qualities as far as possible uncontaminated by learning. This is why so many intelligence tests seem to be so abstract and unrelated to what we usually do. In practice, it is very difficult indeed to assess intelligence without using words, figures or shapes that have at least some familiarity to you. The other side to this equation is that the whole point of measuring IQ is to see whether a person has intelligence that has not yet been developed. It thus provides a measure of how much more a person could achieve, if circumstances could be arranged to permit realization of that person's innate potential.

Aptitude tests may be slightly different from intelligence

tests, because they are designed to assess potential for something specific. For example, rather than assess to what degree a person may be able to think through problems, aptitude tests attempt to assess whether a person can think through problems that are relevant to distinct fields of endeavour. What distinguishes aptitude tests from intelligence tests is that the purpose of aptitude tests is more practical.

The IQ scale

Most IQ scales use the number 100 as an average. People with above average scores, say, up to about 115 on appropriate tests, usually extend their schooling, obtaining vocational and technical qualifications.

People with stronger aptitudes are usually able to apply themselves to degree or professional courses. This group will, roughly, be the intellectual top 10 per cent and have an average IQ of 119.

The top 5 per cent have an IQ around 125. If you are very good at the tests, you may have an IQ of around 135, which puts you into the top 1 per cent.

Remember to interpret your own score only as a general guide. If we assume that you might have a 'true' IQ this will not be revealed unless you are compared with people of the same age, sex and relevant background. It is best to assume that your own IQ from the table provided here is likely to be only a baseline estimate. Use it to ask yourself whether you are achieving what you would expect at college or in your career. What tests should you use to calculate your IQ? It is possible to obtain an IQ on each one of the tests. The fairest estimate is probably to take the sum of several scores, then divide that number by the number of tests you have used.

Your IQ

	UP TO 100	105	110	115	120	125	130	135	140	145
VISUAL	1-6	7-9	10-13	14-17	18-20	21-24	25-26	27-28	29-30	31-32
NUMERICAL	1-4	5	6-7	8-10	11-12	13-16	17	18	19	20
VERBAL	1-7	8-9	10-11	12-13	14-15	16-18	19-20	21-22	23-26	27-33
SEQUENCES	1-8	9-10	11-12	13-16	17-18	19-21	22-24	25-28	29-30	31-32
SPATIAL	1-26	27-30	31-34	35-38	39-42	43-48	49-54	55-60	61-65	66-70
THREE-D	1-12	13-14	15-16	17-18	19-21	22-24	25-26	27-28	29	30
SYSTEMS	1-100	101-116	117-132	133-149	150-165	166-183	184-200	201-208	209-214	215-216
VOCABULARY	1-19	20-22	23-25	26-27	28-30	31-34	35-36	37-38	39	40
FIGUREWORK	1-6	7-9	10-12	13-14	15-18	19-21	22-23	24-25	26-27	28-30

Calculating your 'IQ'

('X' equals the number of tests used.)

Total 'IQ' score
from X tests   = _____

Divide by X tests   / _____

'IQ'   = _____

Part 2

Personality

11

Personality test and job satisfaction

Personality test

Look at each statement in turn. You have to assess yourself in relation to each statement on a scale of 1 to 10.

If you gave yourself a score of 1, this would mean that the statement was not true of you at all.

A score of 10 would mean that the statement described you perfectly. A score of 5 or 6 would mean that the statement is sometimes true for you, and sometimes untrue. Therefore, the larger the score you give yourself, the more you think the statement describes you.

You have to respond to each statement.

There are no right or wrong answers in this test. Your answers will give a picture of how you usually are and the way you generally think and feel.

Tick the number in each scale that is true for you. For the time being, pay no attention to the letter at the end of each row. The letter is to assist you in scoring your results and how to do this will be explained later when you have completed the test.

1. I prefer to be left alone to get on with my work.

1	2	3	4	5	6	7	8	9	10		SO

2. I make myself known to everybody.

1	2	3	4	5	6	7	8	9	10		A

3. I always make sure I get my facts correct.

1	2	3	4	5	6	7	8	9	10		F

4. I can often speak or act without enough thought.

1	2	3	4	5	6	7	8	9	10		SP

5. I cannot get difficulties out of my mind.

1	2	3	4	5	6	7	8	9	10		I

6. I take proper time to prepare for things that might be difficult.

1	2	3	4	5	6	7	8	9	10		D

7. Nobody stops me from speaking if I have something to say.

1	2	3	4	5	6	7	8	9	10		A

8. I like it best when someone else takes the lead.

1	2	3	4	5	6	7	8	9	10		P

9. I do not like to do anything too different from my friends.

1	2	3	4	5	6	7	8	9	10		G

10. I am affected by how people feel.

1	2	3	4	5	6	7	8	9	10		I

11. I make sure that what I do is done as well as it possibly can be.

1	2	3	4	5	6	7	8	9	10		D

12. I am quick to sense people's difficulties.

1	2	3	4	5	6	7	8	9	10		I

13. I like to avoid dealing with feelings if at all possible.

1	2	3	4	5	6	7	8	9	10		F

14. I do not react hastily.

1	2	3	4	5	6	7	8	9	10		D

15. I am at my best when working alongside others.

1	2	3	4	5	6	7	8	9	10		G

16. I do not like going out very much.

1	2	3	4	5	6	7	8	9	10		P

17. To have fun and entertainment in my leisure time is important to me.

| 1 | 2 | 3 | 4 | 5 | 6 | 7 | 8 | 9 | 10 | | SP |

18. I pay no attention to the way others are feeling.

| 1 | 2 | 3 | 4 | 5 | 6 | 7 | 8 | 9 | 10 | | F |

19. I get bored easily.

| 1 | 2 | 3 | 4 | 5 | 6 | 7 | 8 | 9 | 10 | | SP |

20. I am less sensitive than other people.

| 1 | 2 | 3 | 4 | 5 | 6 | 7 | 8 | 9 | 10 | | F |

21. It takes a lot to dent my confidence.

| 1 | 2 | 3 | 4 | 5 | 6 | 7 | 8 | 9 | 10 | | F |

22. Always doing something new and different appeals to me.

| 1 | 2 | 3 | 4 | 5 | 6 | 7 | 8 | 9 | 10 | | SP |

23. A favourite activity of mine is entertaining friends.

| 1 | 2 | 3 | 4 | 5 | 6 | 7 | 8 | 9 | 10 | | G |

24. I control any feelings of annoyance.

| 1 | 2 | 3 | 4 | 5 | 6 | 7 | 8 | 9 | 10 | | P |

25. I always speak my mind.

1	2	3	4	5	6	7	8	9	10		A

26. I can lose sleep because I dwell upon past events.

1	2	3	4	5	6	7	8	9	10		I

27. I do not look for people to be with.

1	2	3	4	5	6	7	8	9	10		SO

28. I am a contented person.

1	2	3	4	5	6	7	8	9	10		D

29. I can easily make decisions by myself.

1	2	3	4	5	6	7	8	9	10		SO

30. I do not like to persuade people to change their minds.

1	2	3	4	5	6	7	8	9	10		P

31. I do not find it difficult to stick at one thing.

1	2	3	4	5	6	7	8	9	10		D

32. I can change my mind at a moment's notice.

1	2	3	4	5	6	7	8	9	10		SP

33. I am often the one who gets people involved when they get together.

1	2	3	4	5	6	7	8	9	10		A

34. I see no harm in passing on confidences to my friends.

1	2	3	4	5	6	7	8	9	10		G

35. People would consider me insightful.

1	2	3	4	5	6	7	8	9	10		I

36. I generally agree if someone feels very strongly about something.

1	2	3	4	5	6	7	8	9	10		P

37. I generally win arguments.

1	2	3	4	5	6	7	8	9	10		A

38. Having friends is not particularly important to me.

1	2	3	4	5	6	7	8	9	10		SO

39. I do not like people to intrude on my space.

1	2	3	4	5	6	7	8	9	10		SO

40. I like people to call me anytime.

1	2	3	4	5	6	7	8	9	10		G

Marking the questionnaire

1. Count up your score for each row marked 'SO'. Do the same for 'G' and for the other letters. Place each total in the score chart below. The example shows you how to do this. The maximum you can have for each letter is 50.

2. With each pair of scores, write in the letter or letters associated with the higher score. This is the dominant letter and is written in the chart on the right-hand side in the place provided.

The scores go together in pairs as follows:

SO and G
A and P
I and F
SP and D

3. The difference between the two scores in each pair should be written in to the extreme right section of the score chart.

Example

Total Scores		Dominant Letter	Score Difference
SO = 25	G = 10	SO	15
A = 18	P = 40	P	22
I = 6	F = 42	F	36
SP = 30	D = 8	SP	22

Write your own scores in the chart below.

Score chart

Total Scores	Dominant Letter	Score Difference
SO = ...	G = ...	....
A = ...	P = ...	.....
I = ...	F = ...	.....
SP = ...	D = ...	.....

Personality chart

You can place your scores in the chart of personality. You mark your score with a cross (X) at the appropriate place. Scoring is from the centre of the graph. Enter your own score on the left or the right of the graph according to your dominant letter. The example below shows you how.

Example

SO Solitary	50 45 40 35 30 25 20 **X** 10	10 15 20 25 30 35 40 45 50	**G** Gregarious
A Assertive	50 45 40 35 30 25 20 15 10	10 15 **X** 25 30 35 40 45 50	**P** Passive
I Imaginative	50 45 40 35 30 25 20 15 10	10 15 20 25 30 **X** 40 45 50	**F** Factual
SP Spontaneous	50 45 40 35 30 25 **X** 15 10	10 15 20 25 30 35 40 45 50	**D** Deliberate

The personality characteristics drawn from the example chart are **SO**, **P**, **F** and **SP**, because these are the dominant letters shown by the score differences.

If your score is borderline

The higher you score for any of the dominant letters, the more noticeably your behaviour will correspond to the description. If your score is borderline, your behaviour may change along that dimension, but may rarely become extremely noticeable. However, you will probably consider that your behaviour is generally more towards one side than the other. Therefore, choose the letter or letters that usually describe your behaviour.

Personality chart

SO	Solitary	50454035302520 15 10	10 1520 253035404550	G	Gregarious
A	Assertive	50454035302520 15 10	10 1520 253035404550	P	Passive
I	Imaginative	50454035302520 15 10	10 1520 253035404550	F	Factual
SP	Spontaneous	50454035302520 15 10	10 1520 253035404550	D	Deliberate

Write in your dominant letters here:

Understanding your personality further

Ask your partner, a friend or colleague to complete the questionnaire for how they perceive you. If the results differ from your own, it could lead to an interesting discussion. It is not that they, or you, are necessarily right or wrong.

In the end, it is up to you which of the results you decide to adopt as the truer representation of yourself. However, where there are differences, it is always enlightening to ask: 1) how different perceptions of you might arise; and also 2) how important these differences might be in career terms.

Although you behave in different ways, depending upon the circumstances you are in or the people you are with, you nevertheless have a personality that remains identifiable. If this were not true, people would not be able to anticipate your reactions; the very fact that there are aspects of you that are predictable testifies to your personality.

This is not to say that your personality will never change. It may well do so, especially if you make efforts to become aware of your potential and give yourself experiences that develop you. However, it seems practical to take your personality as it is now in order to see how it may relate more successfully to one career rather than another.

Different careers do, by and large, require different characteristics. If you work at something that 'suits you' then you will avoid frustration, while your continuing satisfaction and enjoyment are more likely to be assured. It is also true that most careers can be done equally enjoyably by people with widely varying characteristics. It is bound to be so, since no two people are ever completely alike. However, in very broad terms, it makes sense to ask, 'In this career, how would my personality fit?' and, 'Would I enjoy and be successful in this career for the very reason that my personality might be unusual?'

Personality is a complex subject. The aim here is to assist you to assess yourself in relation to some dimensions of personality that are useful in planning your career – what it is about the way you feel and behave that might make you more suited to one career rather than another. To do this, it is best to be honest with yourself as to how you see yourself. There are no rights or wrongs to a test of personality. What is wanted is a description of the real 'you'. Now, just in case you 'undersell' or 'oversell' yourself, you could ask other people who are close to you and know you well to complete the test for the way they see you. If that means you have to photocopy the test it is all right for you to do so for this purpose. Then compare your own responses with that of others.

The most accurate description of 'you' is likely to be the person you are now, the way you behave and the person other people know and recognize. It is possible to answer the test on the basis of assuming how you think you want to be one day, but as you have not got there yet, you will need to think carefully what you have to do to change.

Another factor to consider is whether you might be using only some parts of your personality now, but want to use other parts later on as you develop in your career. For example, if you are factual you might enjoy studying for a scientific career, but later on, if you find yourself working at a laboratory bench, you may find it has too little scope for you if your personality is also gregarious.

Interpretation of your scores

People dimensions

The personality test has two dimensions that describe the way you relate to people: 1) whether you tend to be solitary or gregarious; and 2) whether you tend to be assertive or passive:

SO – SOLITARY

Self-reliant. Takes initiative on his or her own. Shows initiative. May be seen as either quiet or arrogant. 'Outsider' as an extreme. Works in own way. Can socialize but sometimes shy. Not at ease socially. Detached and purposeful.

G – GREGARIOUS

Fits in, not necessarily the leader. Seeks company. Hates to be alone. Loyal and provides support. May be easily persuaded by the group out of need to be accepted. Changes behaviour to fit in. Resolves differences between others. Participative,

Makes up own mind. Re-
sourceful. Does not make
'small talk'.

enjoys making decisions
with others.

archaeologist, farmworker,
chiropodist, interpreter,
delivery person, shepherd,
silversmith, train driver,
writer, craftsperson,
photographer, taxi driver,
programmer

airline cabin staff,
auctioneer, club secretary,
entertainments officer,
house parent, play leader,
publican, sailor, soldier,
youth worker,
trainer

A – ASSERTIVE

P – PASSIVE

Aggressive. May be dominant
and stubborn. Seen as
'pushy'. May talk loudly.
Gets the point across.
Determined, sometimes
risk taking, gets what he or
she wants. Can 'tread on
toes'. May be seen as a 'show
off' but also gains respect.
May lose sight of how people
are affected. Critical.
Demanding. Takes
responsibility.

Keeps matters to
himself/herself. Gives way
rather than argue. Easy to
get on with. Often good
team member.
Accommodating and not
easily annoyed. May avoid
saying what is on his or her
mind. Avoids confrontation.
Tries hard to please.
Cooperative, respectful and
helpful.

broker, club manager, actor,
courier, news editor, sales
agent, hotel manager, fashion
buyer, negotiator, drama
teacher, transport manager,
reporter

bookbinder, computer
operator, dressmaker,
engraver, gamekeeper,
dietician, gardener, potter,
store keeper, technical writer,
patent examiner

Task dimensions

The questionnaire also has two factors that relate to the task:
1) whether you tend to be imaginative or factual; 2) whether
you tend to be spontaneous or deliberate:

I – IMAGINATIVE

Sensitive and aware of
people's feelings. Emotional
and often expressive. Makes
decisions with heart rather
than head. Easily affected,
hurt by criticism. Spends too
much time on small things.
Often discouraged and
frustrated, but also intuitive
and creative. Responsive to
feelings and/or ideas.

artist, author (non-technical),
musician, dancer, florist,
music therapist, speech and
drama teacher, window
dresser

F – FACTUAL

Sees things logically. Usually
composed and has 'feet on
the ground'. Likes orderly,
structured behaviour. Not
easily distracted, does things
in a controlled way.
Objective and analytical, sees
the essential point. May miss
subtle issues that bother
others. Likes information and
facts.

barrister, camera person,
customs officer, diver, estate
agent, mechanic, prison
officer, technician, traffic
warden

SP – SPONTANEOUS

Lively and impulsive. Likes
change and situations which
are fast moving and different.
Often finds it difficult to
stick to one thing or to finish
what he or she has started.
Amusing and enthusiastic, his

D – DELIBERATE

Calm, stable and dependable.
Patient in waiting for things
to take their time. Composed
and unflustered by events.
Takes things as they come.
The slow, deliberate
approach allows people to

or her excitement can infect others. May be seen as lacking 'depth' as he or she chases from one thing to the next. Organization could be forgotten, though he or she might produce a great effect.

depend upon him or her. Could appear dull or unresponsive. Predictable. Smug – the type who says, 'I told you so.' Copes with pressure. Gets things done in an orderly way.

dancer, demonstrator, dresser, hairdresser, advertising assistant, masseur/masseuse, model, public relations assistant, retail assistant, barperson

ambulance crew, administrator, therapist, draughtsperson, ergonomist, firefighter, security officer, osteopath, restorer, surgeon, work study officer

Your orientation towards the task and the manner in which you relate to people have implications for all careers. Not all of the descriptions will necessarily match you exactly, though the general description they give may be important in relation to different areas of work.

Description of personality titles

The personality test provides 16 combinations, based upon the eight descriptions that are formed from the four dimensions. For example, a researcher is solitary, passive, factual and deliberate.

From your own four sets of letters, you can locate yourself in the chart of individual personality titles.

Look first at the top line. Locate yourself to the left or the right of the chart, simply by saying, 'Am I factual or imaginative?' Then, looking at the bottom line of the chart, ask yourself, 'Am I deliberate or spontaneous?' This will locate you in one of the four columns.

You repeat the procedure by looking at the rows. Looking at the left-hand side of the chart, ask yourself, 'Am I gregarious or solitary?' Then from the right-hand side of the chart, 'Am I assertive or passive?' You will now have located yourself in one of the 16 boxes.

Remember that you are more clearly in one area than another if your scores are more at the extreme end of each dimension. Where your scores are around the middle range, you may consider that, on balance, an adjacent area might be more like you. For example, in the chart below, number 13, a researcher, might be number 9, an arranger, if he or she is a little more assertive.

Chart of individual personality titles

TASK	Factual	Factual	Imaginative	Imaginative	PEOPLE
Gregarious	1. Director	2. Opportunist	3. Coach	4. Crusader	Assertive
Gregarious	5. Completer	6. Associate	7. Confidant	8. Colleague	Passive
Solitary	9. Arranger	10. Adviser	11. Designer	12. Idealist	Assertive
Solitary	13. Researcher	14. Implementer	15. Specialist	16. Wanderer	Passive
PEOPLE	Deliberate	Spontaneous	Deliberate	Spontaneous	Task

My dominant letters, from the personality chart, were:

1. FDAG – Director
Characteristics: Factual, Deliberate, Assertive and Gregarious
Careers: armed forces officer, bank manager, general manager, hotel manager, production manager, retail manager, transport manager

2. FSpAG – Opportunist
Characteristics: Factual, Spontaneous, Assertive and Gregarious
Careers: advertising executive, auctioneer, club secretary, estate agent, public relations director, politician, sports coach or manager, senior administrator, funds organizer

3. IDAG – Coach
Characteristics: Imaginative, Deliberate, Assertive and Gregarious
Careers: doctor, osteopath, psychologist, senior nursing officer, senior teacher, social worker, youth worker

4. ISpAG – Crusader
Characteristics: Imaginative, Spontaneous, Assertive and Gregarious
Careers: civil rights worker, courier, beautician, demonstrator, journalist, public relations executive, drama teacher, union representative

5. FDPG – Completer
Characteristics: Factual, Deliberate, Passive and Gregarious
Careers: ambulance crew, armed forces, cashier, nurse, police officer, prison officer, firefighter, guard

6. *FSpPG – Associate*
Characteristics: Factual, Spontaneous, Passive and Gregarious
Careers: air hostess or steward, bar person, dental assistant, hairdresser, play leader, junior teacher, secretary, sports or gym assistant, team leader

7. *IDPG – Confidant*
Characteristics: Imaginative, Deliberate, Passive and Gregarious
Careers: hospital porter, house parent, mental nurse, nursery teacher, remedial teacher, social worker, therapist

8. *ISpPG – Colleague*
Characteristics: Imaginative, Spontaneous, Passive and Gregarious
Careers: counsellor, marketing assistant, nursery nurse, receptionist, retail assistant, stage hand, waiter/waitress

9. *FDASo – Arranger*
Characteristics: Factual, Deliberate, Assertive and Solitary
Careers: barrister, police inspector, solicitor, work study officer, customs officer, tax inspector

10. *FSpASo – Adviser*
Characteristics: Factual, Spontaneous, Assertive and Solitary
Careers: importer/exporter, buyer, entrepreneur, commodities or futures broker, sales director, market trader, property speculator, road manager, club manager

11. *IDASo – Designer*
Characteristics: Imaginative, Deliberate, Assertive and Solitary
Careers: analyst, architect, business consultant, inspector, journalist, librarian, social scientist, medical scientist

12. ISpASo – Idealist
Characteristics: Imaginative, Spontaneous, Assertive and Solitary
Careers: architect, artist, author, chef, dancer, interior designer, musician, sculptor

13. FDPSo – Researcher
Characteristics: Factual, Deliberate, Passive and Solitary
Careers: accounting technician, actuary, archivist, auditor, driver, engineer, reinsurer, operations researcher

14. FSpPSo – Implementer
Characteristics: Factual, Spontaneous, Passive and Solitary
Careers: accounting technician, tour guide, cook, dietician, interpreter, computer technician, paramedic, road patrol officer, surgeon

15. IDPSo – Specialist
Characteristics: Imaginative, Deliberate, Passive and Solitary
Careers: arborist, curator, farm worker, site worker, gardener, historian, delivery person, potter, shepherd, thatcher, saddler, gun-maker, planner

16. ISpPSo – Wanderer
Characteristic: Imaginative, Spontaneous, Passive and Solitary
Careers: bar person, dancer, disc jockey, entertainer, model, porter, production worker, shop assistant, waiter/waitress

Part 3

Motivation

12

Career search test

Instructions

This is a broad, general test, which looks at all types and levels of occupations.

You are given three careers in each line of the test. You have to choose the one that appeals to you first, second and last. It is necessary to make a choice between all three so that a complete picture can be built up. When you do not know what a particular career entails, it is a good idea to look it up in a directory of occupations.

When looking at each set of three, simply write 1, 2 and 3 in the place provided, as in the example you are given on the next page. Sometimes you will find a set where the items are equally attractive or unattractive. Nevertheless, you have to make a choice in each case.

Important: The test seeks to establish what career areas appeal to you. However, some people are concerned about how to respond if there is a distinction between what might appeal to them and what they think they are realistically capable of doing. There are two ways in which you can respond to the items in the test. Firstly, you could respond by asking yourself: 'Would I like to do this career, regardless of whether I think I have the ability or qualifications?' This is generally the preferred method.

Secondly, you could respond by asking yourself: 'Would I like to do this job and am I capable?' If you prefer to respond to the test in this way, that is perfectly all right; you can always do the test the other way later, using the first approach, if you wish.

Remember also that there is a danger of thinking you cannot do something when in fact you do have the hidden potential.

Above the sets of activities or jobs you have to choose between you will see the letters W, A, P, E, O, B and S. Ignore these for the time being. They will help with scoring your answers later on.

Example

Place these jobs in order of your preference:

		W	A	P	E	O	B	S
a)	Animal worker			a **3**				
b)	Laboratory assistant				b **1**			
c)	Chemist's shop owner						c **2**	

In the example, being a laboratory assistant is preferred most, then owning a chemist's shop, while being an animal worker is least preferred.

The test is done in just the same way. Begin when you are ready.

Career search test

	W	A	P	E	O	B	S
1 a) Journalist	a						
b) Architect		b					
c) Security guard			c				
2 a) Dress maker		a					
b) Gym instructor			b				
c) Geophysicist				c			
3 a) Bus driver			a				
b) Dietician				b			
c) Administrative assistant					c		
4 a) Medical technical officer				a			
b) Call centre adviser					b		
c) Business person						c	
5 a) Arrange loans for banking customers					a		
b) Market research executive						b	
c) Hospital nurse							c
6 a) Copy writer	a						
b) Sculptor		b					
c) Medical laboratory scientist			c				
Leave this row blank until test is completed							

	W	A	P	E	O	B	S
7 a) Sign writer		a					
b) Tree pruner (Arborist)			b				
c) Purchasing officer					c		
8 a) Barperson			a				
b) Computer systems programmer				b			
c) Commodity broker						c	
9 a) Ecologist				a			
b) Business statistician					b		
c) Teacher of the blind							c
10 a) Actor/actress	a						
b) Furniture designer		b					
c) Post office clerical worker					c		
11 a) Graphic designer		a					
b) Window cleaner			b				
c) Head of a charity					c		
12 a) Building worker			a				
b) Orthodontist				b			
c) Osteopath							c
Leave this row blank until test is completed							

	W	A	P	E	O	B	S
13 a) Biochemist				a			
b) Antique dealer						b	
c) Drugs counsellor							c
14 a) Film critic	a						
b) Jewellery designer		b					
c) Art dealer						c	
15 a) Choral singer		a					
b) Jockey			b				
c) Educational psychologist							c
16 a) Production manager			a				
b) Company secretary					b		
c) Merchant banker						c	
17 a) Linguist	a						
b) Organist		b					
c) Prison officer							c
18 a) Member of a music band		a					
b) Scientific instrument technician				b			
c) Legal assistant					c		
Leave this row blank until test is completed							

	W	A	P	E	O	B	S
19 a) Member of a lifeboat crew			a				
b) Purchasing officer					b		
c) Residential social worker							c
20 a) Children's author	a						
b) Traffic warden			b				
c) Doctor of medicine				c			
21 a) Book cover/poster artist		a					
b) Veterinary surgeon				b			
c) Property dealer						c	
22 a) Gun maker			a				
b) Hotel owner						b	
c) Careers adviser							c
23 a) Librarian	a						
b) Truck driver			b				
c) Court reporter					c		
24 a) Photographer		a					
b) Astronomer			b				
c) Naturopath							c
Leave this row blank until test is completed							

	W	A	P	E	O	B	S
25 a) Advertising copywriter	a						
b) Cook			b				
c) Publicity agent						c	
26 a) Window dresser		a					
b) Invoice payments manager					b		
c) Account manager						c	
27 a) Bookseller	a						
b) Electrical engineer			b				
c) Children's nurse							c
28 a) Interior decorator		a					
b) Trading standards officer					b		
c) Remedial teacher							c
29 a) Local newspaper reporter	a						
b) Pharmacist			b				
c) Statistician					c		
30 a) Art restorer		a					
b) Management consultant						b	
c) Physiotherapist							c
Leave this row blank until test is completed							

	W	A	P	E	O	B	S
31 a) Technical author	a						
b) Anthropologist				b			
c) Shop owner						c	

	W	A	P	E	O	B	S
32 a) Newsreader	a						
b) Bacteriologist				b			
c) Youth club leader							c

	W	A	P	E	O	B	S
33 a) Proof-reader	a						
b) Tax adviser					b		
c) Insurance salesperson						c	

	W	A	P	E	O	B	S
34 a) Language teacher	a						
b) Banking adviser					b		
c) Teacher of the deaf							c

	W	A	P	E	O	B	S
35 a) Television programme researcher	a						
b) Share trader						b	
c) Social worker							c

Leave this row blank until test is completed							

Scoring

Step 1: Add column totals on each page of the test and place in the last box on each page. Place all page totals below:

	W	A	P	E	O	B	S
COLUMN TOTALS/all pages							

Step 2: Convert your score to a percentage (%) score, from the table given below:

%		100	95	90	85	80	75	70	65	60	55
score		15	16–17	18	19–20	21	22–23	24	25–26	27	28–29
%		50	45	40	35	30	25	20	15	10	5
score		30	31–32	33	34–35	36	37–38	39	40–41	42	43–45

For example, a score of 15 on W, or on any of the letters, would give a percentage score of 100. A score of 21 would give a percentage of 80. A score of 44 would give a percentage of 5.

Step 3: Place percentage scores in the columns:

	W	A	P	E	O	B	S
Percentage score (%)							

Step 4: Make a mark with a pen or pencil at the point on the chart to show where your percentage score lies on each line. Connect up each of the points. For example, for the following percentage scores:

	W	A	P	E	O	B	S
Percentage score (%)	15	10	90	5	60	20	10

The chart would look like this:

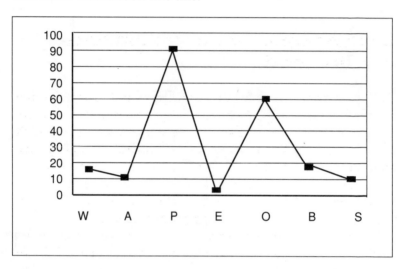

Motivation and careers chart

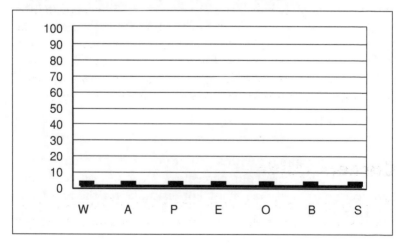

This is what the letters mean:

W	A	P	E	O	B	S
Words	Art	Physical	Experimental	Organizational	Business	Social

Interpretation of motivation and careers chart

The chart shows your areas of preferred and least preferred types of work. A single high score will show very clearly where your motivation lies. If there is another almost equally high score, or another strong score, you will probably want to have some chance of using this area of motivation in your work as well. Also look at your lowest scores, because these are the least important to you, so you are unlikely to enjoy a career so much if it places undue emphasis on these areas.

It is usually possible to find a career combining more than one area of motivation. Indeed, most careers demand more than one interest.

If your chart does not have any outstanding areas of interest this will mean either that you are motivated by everything, or that none of the areas appeal to you at all! Either result could mean you want a very broad job that involves you in some way with everything that is going on. In this case, it is probably a good idea to take the test again and this time be strict with yourself about what is realistically possible for you.

Careers guide

If you have more than a single strong area of interest, try to find a way to involve all of your interests in a career. Although it is often necessary to specialize, there are often opportunities to 'bolt on' other interests to your main career. For example, an architect may have a strong interest in the Art area, but some architects may also be interested in involving themselves in Business and Organization. Similarly, an accountant is likely to have a strong interest in the Organization area. If there is also an interest in the Social area, it may be possible to take responsibility for human resources matters within an accounting business. If there is an interest in the Physical area, it may be possible to work out of doors, perhaps in quantity surveying, or work in an organization that deals with products, equipment or machines.

The examples that are given below are those that often correspond with an area of interest.

W – Words
actor/actress
advertising copywriter
bilingual secretary
book critic
creative writer
editor
historian
interpreter
journalist
language teacher
librarian
literary critic
proof-reader

A – Art
architect
artist
dancer
dressmaker

engraver
florist
goldsmith
illustrator
interior designer
make-up artist
musician
sculptor
silversmith
vision mixer
window dresser

P – Physical

agricultural mechanic
animal handler
appliance repairer
automobile technician
baker
blacksmith/farrier
boat builder
builder
butcher
carpenter
coastguard
cook
diver
driver
farmer
fisherman
fitter
forester
gamekeeper
groom
groundsman
guard

gunsmith
instrument maker
jockey
joiner
lighthouse keeper
locksmith
mechanic
merchant seaman
miner
nature conservancy warden
oil rig worker
park ranger
plumber
shipping pilot
traffic warden
upholsterer
veterinary nurse

E – Experimenting

astronomer
audiology technician
bacteriologist
botanist
chemist
dietician
ergonomist
experimental psychologist
forensic scientist
laboratory technician
materials scientist
mathematician
meteorologist
microbiologist
ophthalmologist
physicist

radiographer
surgeon
zoologist

O – Organization
accountant
accounting technician
actuary
administrator
auditor
bank clerk
bursar
cashier
clerk
company secretary
fund manager/assistant
legal executive
purser
records clerk
securities analyst
tax inspector

B – Business
broker
business consultant
business person
exporter/importer
management consultant
managing director
marketing manager
negotiator
personnel director
political agent
politician

retail manager
sales manager

S – Social
ambulance crew
careers adviser
child-care officer
chiropodist
educational psychologist
health visitor
hostel warden
industrial nurse
medical practitioner
midwife
nurse
nursery nurse
osteopath
physiotherapist
probation officer
remedial teacher
social worker
teacher

Social and words
drama teacher
interviewer
language teacher
liberal studies teacher
psychoanalyst
speech therapist
training officer

Words and art
actor/actress

advertising copywriter
dramatist
film director
film reviewer
TV production assistant
voice-over

Art and physical
bookbinder
cabinet maker
cake maker
camera person
confectioner
curtain maker
dresser
embalmer
emboiderer
flyperson
gardener
pattern cutter
pattern maker
picture framer
potter

Physical and experimenting
agriculturist
biomedical engineer
computer engineer
engineer
– aeronautical
– civil
– mechanical
– production
environmental health officer
ergonomist

geologist
horologist
hydrologist
instrument maker
metallurgist
navigating officer
surveyor
technologist
work study officer

Experimenting and organizing
business systems analyst
chief actuary
computer programmer
economist
market researcher
operations researcher
statistician
systems analyst

Organizing and business
bank manager
club manager
estate manager
insurance manager
office manager
tax consultant
turf accountant
underwriter

Business and social
charity manager
funeral director

head teacher
hospital manager
hotel manager
job interviewer
retail manager
salesperson
social services director

Social and art
aromatherapist
art teacher
art therapist
beautician
dance instructor
masseur/masseuse
music therapist
nursery teacher
occupational therapist
piano teacher
waiter/waitress

Social and physical
hairdresser
masseur/masseuse
occupational therapist
police officer
prison officer
production supervisor
sports coach/assistant
team coach
youth leader

Social and experimenting
clinical psychologist

dental assistant
dentist
nurse
orthoptist
radiographer
science teacher
social science researcher

Words and physical
printer
secretary in agriculture
sports writer
technical writer

Art and experimenting
archaeologist
beautician
car stylist
cartographer
designer
fine art restorer
lighting technician
medical illustrator
museum assistant
photographer

Physical and organizing
baths manager
builder's merchant
customs officer
manufacturing team leader
logistics manager/transport manager
office machinery mechanic
organization and methods officer

rating valuation officer
works manager

Physical and business
accident assessor
auctioneer
demonstrator
domestic engineering manager
estate agent
farm manager
production manager
publican
undertaker

Experimenting and business
computer consultant
director of scientific research company
dispensing optician
medical representative
retail pharmacist
technical representative
veterinary surgeon

Experimenting and words
anthropologist
archaeologist
information scientist
market researcher
science writer
technical writer

Organizing and social
courier/local representative
employment officer

medical secretary
principal nursing officer

Organizing and words
administrator (clerical/executive)
barrister
company secretary
entertainment officer
legal executive
library assistant
receptionist
secretary
solicitor

Organizing and art
box office clerk
chef
choreographer
cinema manager
front of house manager
merchandiser
props manager
receptionist
studio assistant
theatre administrator
wardrobe manager

Business and words
conference executive
literary agent
newspaper editor/manager
public relations executive
publisher
radio, TV or film producer

Business and art
advertising account executive
art dealer
brand manager
fashion buyer
media director
salesperson

Career development test

Instructions

This test provides extra information to people who are already in a career, but want to review or extend it. It is also suitable for people who want to work at a professional or managerial level.

With each item you are given three activities and you have to choose the one that appeals to you first, second and last. It is necessary to make a choice between all three so that a complete picture can be built up. When looking at each set of three, simply write 1, 2 and 3 in the place provided, as in the example you are given below. Sometimes you will find a set where the items are equally attractive or unattractive. Nevertheless, you have to make a choice in each case.

Important: the test seeks to establish what sorts of activities appeal to you. However, some people are concerned about how to respond if there is a distinction between what might appeal to them and what they think they are realistically capable of doing. There are two ways in which you can respond to the items in the test. Firstly, you could respond by asking yourself, 'Would I like to do this activity, regardless of whether I think I have the ability or qualifications?' This is generally the preferred method. Second, you could respond by asking yourself, 'Would I like to do this activity and am I capable?' If you prefer to respond to the questionnaire in this way that is perfectly satisfactory; you can always do the questionnaire the other way later, using the first approach, if you wish.

Remember, also, that there is a danger of thinking you cannot do something when in fact you do have the hidden potential.

Next to each activity you will see the letters W, A, P, E, O, B and S. Ignore these for the time being. They will help with scoring your answers later on.

Example

Place each set of three activities in order. To the right of each activity mark 1, 2 or 3 corresponding to your first, second and third preference:

a)	Attend to the health of farm animals	3	P
b)	Investigate causes of disease	1	E
c)	Manage a shop	2	B

In the example, investigating the causes of diseases is preferred most, then managing a shop, while attending to the health of farm animals is least preferred. If this copy of the book does not belong to you, simply write down your answers on a spare piece of paper.

The test is done in just the same way as the example. Begin when you are ready.

Career development test

1.

a)	Teach a language (be an interpreter)	W
b)	Decide upon framing and composition for filming	A
c)	Manage a section of a factory that produces car parts	P

2.

a)	Play in an orchestra	A
b)	Project manage new production machinery	P
c)	Identify remnants from ancient burial sites	E

3.

a)	Supervise the introduction of drilling equipment for oil	P
b)	Use computers to approximate human intelligence	E
c)	Calculate the risk of insurance premiums	O

4.

a)	Study diseases of plants	E
b)	Give advice about financial policies	O
c)	Form a marketing strategy for pop music	B

5.

a)	Estimate the cost of damage by fire or flood	O
b)	Run an advertising promotion	B
c)	Be consulted by patients as a health expert	S

6.

a)	Translate speeches from one language to another	W
b)	Design houses	A
c)	Research how food can be preserved and stored	E

7.

a)	Write music for television commercials	A
b)	Work from drawings to make engineering parts	P
c)	Analyse the financial policy of a business	O

8.

a) Survey an area of country for the construction   P
   of a new road
b) Study scientific journals to keep up to date with   E
   research
c) Direct the way a business is run   B

9.

a) Study minerals   E
b) Buy and sell stocks on behalf of investors   O
c) Diagnose educational requirements for a   S
   handicapped person

10.

a) Edit articles for inclusion in a magazine   W
b) Draw cartoons for newspapers   A
c) Organize and cost supplies and services   O

11.

a) Talk to people about art   A
b) Manage a farm   P
c) Seek election for political office   B

12.

a) Navigate a vessel at sea   P
b) Take atmospheric readings and record data   E
c) Provide mental therapy for hospital patients   S

13.

a) Develop new instruments for satellite weather   E
   forecasting
b) Look for skilled people for hire by other businesses   B
c) Counsel people in respect of illness or rehabilitation S

14.

a)	Write a book about a historical figure	W
b)	Communicate visually using drawings and photographs	A
c)	Manage a chain of shops	B

15.

a)	Design pottery or ornaments	A
b)	Manage a contract haulage fleet of vehicles	P
c)	Help people to relax to assist well-being	S

16.

a)	Manage others in woodland cultivation and harvesting	P
b)	Compile documents relating to hospital patients	O
c)	Be the chairperson of a committee to raise money for a charity	B

17.

a)	Write a fictional account of a historical event	W
b)	Design and make original articles of clothing	A
c)	Undertake developmental checks on babies	S

18.

a)	Photograph weddings, sporting events and other occasions	A
b)	Use statistical techniques to monitor contamination	E
c)	Estimate the cost of rebuilding damaged property	O

19.

a)	Implement engineering drawings on a construction site	P
b)	Give legal or pensions advice	O
c)	Treat people with language or speech defects	S

20.
a) Teach drama at a college   W
b) Schedule engineers and others on a building project   P
c) Develop new telecommunication systems   E

21.
a) Be responsible for the interior decoration of a boat   A
b) Study ancient documents   E
c) Collect commission on objects you sell for people   B

22.
a) Examine the way tasks are performed to increase   P
    efficiency
b) Run a flat letting agency   B
c) Find families who may be suitable foster parents   S

23.
a) Write scripts for radio programmes   W
b) Be responsible for industrial plant or machinery   P
    for a brewing process
c) Prepare agendas and record minutes of meetings   O

24.
a) Write a book on painting and drawing technique   A
b) Write scientific textbooks   E
c) Advise on options for employment or further   S
    training of young people

25.
a) Manage a theatrical production   W
b) Supervise contractors on the maintenance of an   P
    aircraft
c) Manage a public relations agency   B

26.
a) Design prints and posters   A
b) Advise clients about their tax liabilities   O
c) Acquire start-up businesses requiring investment   B
   and strategy

27.
a) Teach a foreign language   W
b) Teach engineering   P
c) Report on the best arrangement for the care and   S
   custody of children

28.
a) Teach a course in modern art appreciation   A
b) Maintain stock control using necessary software   O
c) Train students to apply psychological techniques   S

29.
a) Write a brochure for advertising a product or event   W
b) Catalogue and index scientific information   E
c) Submit a cost analysis for materials required for a   O
   project

30.
a) Design fashion articles for the clothing industry   A
b) Be a manager in an insurance underwriting business   B
c) Run the training department for a large company   S

31.
a) Read scripts for grammatical and spelling errors   W
b) Communicate scientific information to   E
   non-specialists
c) Buy art works for investment   B

32.
a) Write short articles for magazines   W
b) Research genetic material in a laboratory   E
c) Determine policy for the recruitment and retention   S
    of staff

33.
a) Write about cultural events for a newspaper   W
b) Report on the financial performance of a company   O
c) Buy property for investment or commercial   B

34.
a) Edit scripts prior to publication   W
b) Prepare tax returns for businesses   O
c) Counsel people who have had emotional trauma   S

35.
a) Write press statements communicating business   W
    policies
b) Invest your own money in a franchise   B
c) Visit disadvantaged people to ensure they are being   S
    cared for

Scoring

Step 1: Add totals against each capital letter and place totals below the letters:

	W	A	P	E	O	B	S
Letter totals:							

Step 2: Convert your score to a percentage (%) score from the table given below:

%	100	95	90	85	80	75	70	65	60	55
score	15	16–17	18	19–20	21	22–23	24	25–26	27	28–29
%	50	45	40	35	30	25	20	15	10	5
score	30	31–32	33	34–35	36	37–38	39	40–41	42	43–45

For example, a score of 38 on W, or any of the letters, would give a percentage score of 25. A score of 21 would give a percentage of 80.

Step 3: Place percentage scores below each letter.

	W	A	P	E	O	B	S
Percentage score (%)							

Step 4: Make a mark with a pen or pencil at the point on each of the radiating lines in the chart on page 186 to show where your percentage score lies on each line. Connect up each of the points on the graph. As an example, the next chart has been drawn for the following percentage scores:

	W	A	P	E	O	B	S
Percentage score (%)	5	10	30	15	60	20	70

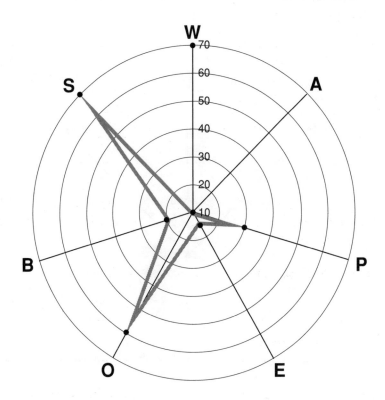

Note that the chart range ends at 70%. This is because any score above this level will indicate a high level of interest. If you have a score that is higher than 70%, you can extend the chart yourself, marking in your score as appropriate.

Motivation chart

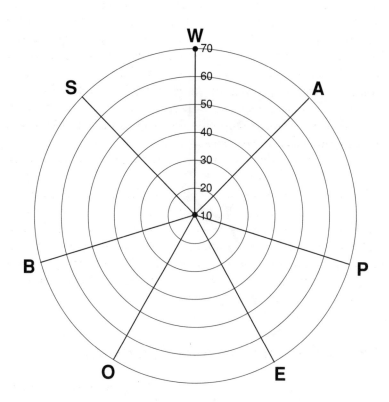

Here is what the letters mean:

W	A	P	E	O	B	S
Words	Art	Physical	Experimental	Organizational	Business	Social

Interpretation of your results

The following information also appears in Chapter 12, but must be repeated here. The chart shows your areas of preferred and least preferred types of work activity. If you have a single high score, this will show very clearly where your motivation lies. If there is another almost equally high score, or another strong score, you will probably want to have some chance of using this area of motivation in your work as well. Also look at your lowest scores, because these are the least important to you, so you are unlikely to enjoy a career so much if it places undue emphasis on these areas.

It is usually possible to find a career that combines more than one area of motivation.

If your chart does not have any outstanding areas of interest, this means either that you are motivated by everything, or that none of the areas appeal to you at all! Either result could mean you want a very broad job that involves you in some way with everything that is going on. In this case, it is probably a good idea to take the test again and this time be strict with yourself about what is realistically possible for you.

Areas for career development

There follows a short description of the main areas of career development opportunity. Some of the possibilities given may have been placed under several of the headings. For example, business administration could appear under either 'Organization' or 'Executive'. Therefore, the category in which you find the courses is designed to give only general guidance. You can also relate your specific areas of motivation to specific jobs by referring to the career profiles in the last chapter of this book.

W: Words

You will use words in your career whatever you do. In fact, you will already be an expert in the use of words simply from your experience of everyday living. However, if this is your high preference, it means that you want to make the business of words the means of making your living, not as an adjunct to some other activity.

You may have enjoyed English or other 'wordy' subjects, such as history, at school. Your aim may be to use words creatively or you may be drawn towards careers which in some way involve you with information and communication.

Few people have the talent to make a living on the basis of their creative writing. More structured and predictable careers arise in journalism or public relations. There are other careers that are often suited to this area of preference, such as legal work and librarianship.

A: Art

A preference in this area almost invariably indicates that you want to use your imagination and express yourself through art, music or dance. At a deeper level, it can often suggest, even though a person may not be artistically gifted, that he or she wants a career which allows freedom and the opportunity to use intuition.

Whatever form of art you pursue is likely to involve plenty of hard work and dedication. The discipline required by artists is frequently unappreciated by those outside artistic professions. Also, many careers in art are relatively lowly paid, which is surprising in view of the length of time needed to study for qualifications.

There are some people who are fortunate enough to become popular with comparatively little effort. So much in this area depends upon 'what the public wants' and whether you happen to be 'at the right place at the right time'.

Most creative careers do not carry any guarantees of security and income. Your employment may depend on the piece of work you produce or may be linked to a short contract. More security of tenure exists if you work on a permanent basis as a member of a design team in a shop, with a manufacturer or in some other organization. These opportunities also give you a more continuing contact with others. This is an important point, since many artists are prepared to follow a style of life that requires a great deal of self-reliance.

P: Physical

This area covers work that involves physical activity, perhaps engaged in sport or working outdoors. At one end of the spectrum, physical work might be delicate, even artistic, while at the other it might be heavy, involving large equipment or machinery. It might require skills that are visual as well as mechanical.

If you score highly in this area it is likely that you want to achieve something concrete. You might want to work by yourself on a task involving materials. Alternatively, you may want to use your experience and common sense in understanding and interacting with the environment. In this case, you may want to work alone and be prepared to do so, often under harsh, sometimes dangerous conditions.

E: Experimental

What probably appeals to you about this area is the opportunity to acquire knowledge and to analyse results. These interests suit you to science since you enjoy observing, recording and making deductions.

Careers in this area require habits of study and precise work. An ability with mathematics is the common link with most, although if your interest is biology you may be less mathematically grounded than if your interest is physics. Work in all the sciences is changing as rapidly as technology changes, so that new opportunities for experimentation arise through increasingly powerful computers. Although science appears to be dependent on instrumentation, it still requires the same enthusiastic curiosity.

Many areas of science are desperately short of qualified people while in others it is difficult to get a job even with a higher degree.

O: Organization

This area is about administration. It includes financial matters as well as legal ones. It is relevant to all institutions whether in the public or private sector, since it involves the effective use of resources, including both people and materials.

Since this area is concerned with making sure that decisions are carried out properly, you will need to coordinate the efforts of others. Your own approach will need to be structured and orderly. People who organize, whether it is in a small office or a large enterprise, often have enormous influence, simply because they are the ones who know most about what is going on. As a consequence, such positions also carry a good deal of responsibility as well. This is why qualifications are increasingly sought in aspirants for senior positions. However, it is still possible to learn through experience and there is no doubt that if you have the right potential you will get on. In the larger organizations, senior positions are most likely to be occupied by people who have professional qualifications in banking, insurance, accountancy or a similar field.

B: Business

If this is your highest preference you will be motivated by the chance to earn your living your own way. It is not about working by yourself, but working for yourself. This is true, even if your business involves running somebody else's business on their behalf. Without a doubt, people who are most successful in this area run the business as if it is their own, whether it is or not. The responsibility and rewards for this type of career include all the attendant risks associated with failing to live up to the expectations people have of you and the specified or assumed promises you have made to them. For sure, in this career you are expected to have personal qualities of drive and determination.

The especially attractive feature of this area is that it is open to anybody, regardless of qualifications, although leaders of large business almost always seek to acquire qualifications in order to improve their performance further. Whatever the size of business you work in, being able to spot an opportunity, together with the will to succeed, are still the essential attributes.

S: Social

Although every career involves contact with others at some point, your objective is to make people your focus. A high score in this area reveals how much you are prepared to assist others in their development. Your career may range from giving advice to devotedly caring for people who are unable to help themselves.

Such careers are seldom easy and sometimes require an extreme measure of personal resourcefulness. For example, social workers who have the best of intentions sometimes have to make decisions on behalf of others which cause stress to everybody concerned, whether professional or client. Before entering a career in this area it is as well to gain experience to make sure it is right for you.

Success in this area depends on personal judgement. Tact, patience and understanding are commodities you must have in abundance. A tough skin is often required in situations where you may receive few thanks for your efforts. Of course, the rewards of seeing people improve make these careers worthwhile.

Social and Words

You will be interested in careers that combine ideas, people and communications. Obvious possibilities are in teaching, although other areas might involve you in some form of business: for example, public relations.

If you are more concerned with the literary side, then language skills may be more important to you than the caring, social side. On the other hand, a speech therapist may have skills in linguistics, although the primary aim is to help others overcome difficulties rather than acquire knowledge.

Words and Art

You appear to seek knowledge and the chance to express ideas, often in novel ways. It is unlikely that you will be satisfied by a more conventional career. Therefore, the way you work and what you do will often be admired by others who value the variety and lifestyle you appear to have. Such careers are not without risk so perhaps the most important asset to have is a belief in yourself and what you are doing.

Art and Physical

This area gives you the chance to apply art in a practical way. An example is a potter, whose sense of proportion and design is wedded to a useful object. There are many crafts that combine beauty with practicality.

There are also attendant opportunities if you look beyond the task itself. For example, your talent might lead to a business, or it could take you into the Social area, through teaching or therapy.

Physical and Experimental

This area will involve you with the application of science. You are the person who takes the theory and makes it work in practice. Such careers demand knowledge and experience. Often, people rely upon you more than they know, and what you do is essential to a secure and comfortable existence.

Experimenting and Organizational

You may be interested in mathematics, statistics, finance or marketing, and other areas that combine your interest in figures with an analytical approach. If your interest is statistics, you are more likely to be on the scientific side. If your interest veers more towards the actuarial, then you will probably prefer to work in a business organization.

Careers that combine the two areas very well indeed, and where there are expanding opportunities, are in the systems field. It is possible to be involved with systems integration as well as systems development within organizations. In these cases, you would be expected to have skills on the Social side as well.

Organizational and Business

You are likely to be astute and commercially minded. You will enjoy the thought of working within organizations such as banking, insurance, finance and administration. You will need to be a good manager, first of all in managing the efforts of others and also in managing systems and resources. Whereas many business-minded people are quite intuitive, you are more controlled and factual. Your knowledge about how businesses work, together with your drive for efficiency, are likely to mean you are a force to be reckoned with.

Business and Social

You will want to work with and for people, but not in a personal, caring way. Instead, your efforts are likely to be more detached, though sometimes on a grander scale. Thus, you might achieve a great deal for others through your business sense. You may show your concern by creating the circumstances or the resources through which others are enabled to care in a more direct way. You are more likely to head the committee that obtains the resources patients need, than be a skilled helper yourself. Your obvious talents are more likely to be political than sensitive, though there is no doubt that the latter is present as well.

Social and Art

Careers that combine these areas require skills in relation to the subject and skills in relation to people. A great deal of sympathy, warmth and patience are required in order to communicate with others and help them. Many careers in this area are undertaken by volunteers, who often have extensive experience and insight to bring to their work. This is unlikely to be the correct area for you if your aim is to do great things with your art. Instead, you should want to use your subject in the service of others, a very selfless activity.

Social and Physical

You want to be active, working with others in order to achieve a definite task. Your tendency is to 'go for it'. The way you approach your work will depend on whether you are something of an Organizer or whether you are more artistic. In the former case, you may be drawn to areas of industrial production. In the latter case, you may enjoy sports coaching or aerobics teaching. If your other, supporting interests are more towards business, then you may like to be in charge of some team work or operation management. Your enthusiasm and ability to work with others usually mean you will be an effective leader.

Social and Experimenting

If these are your interests, you will probably want to apply expert knowledge in the service of others. You may well be consulted for advice, but your relationship with others is more likely to be professional and detached than emotionally involved. Your background will be in science, but your intention will be to direct that science to others' welfare or education.

Words and Physical

These two areas are generally mutually exclusive; although most of us are active and communicating with each other most of the time, there are few careers which combine these two inclinations specifically. The writer of technical books and the sports writer are examples of how the two can come together, but these are very highly specialized careers indeed. How can you get started? It will be worth looking at the Words and Physical areas separately, at the same time thinking whether any careers in these areas will give you enough scope for your other interest. Also, consult the Career database where some other alternatives may be found.

Art and Experimental

You will want scope in your career to combine your interests in an expressive medium as well as analyse. Clearly, you have a desire to use science and technology to create something of perfection. You may well come up with some innovative ideas yourself. It seems that whatever work you do, some creative or technical challenge is important.

Physical and Organizational

If these are your interests, then you will want a career which requires you to implement and get things done. You probably like to work in a moving environment. You may like to be 'out and about' yourself. Ensuring that resources, goods or equipment are getting to the right place at the right time is something which you will be interested in. Increasingly, careers in this area will involve you in costing and budgeting in order that deadlines can be completed on schedule.

Physical and Business

You want to combine an interest in business with the chance to be out and about, or become actively involved with what is happening. You may like to be on a site or involved with property. You might enjoy buying and selling equipment or stock. Typically, you will be practically minded, making things happen or turning your hand to most things.

Experimental and Business

These preferences seek to combine the intellectual with the material. The combination is sometimes possible, as is shown by the number of chemists (pharmacists) who venture into retail. Of course, science is big business, many of the largest companies, such as drug companies, having huge teams of scientific researchers. Those who make it to the top of these organizations start out in science, but have developed a strong streak of business enterprise along the way.

Your interests lie in the realm of ideas, communication and intellectual challenge. You will like to acquire knowledge for which you may perceive novel applications. You may lack the practicality to turn ideas into reality, but you may inspire others to do so.

Organizational and Social

You want to work with others as part of an efficient team. People may well look to you for leadership, since you appear willing to do the necessary paperwork and scheduling. Although your administrative and personal skills may be useful in most organizations, particularly in business, you seem likely to derive most satisfaction when your work has an altruistic element. You work well in a community or public institution where you experience a sense of purpose from assisting others.

It may be that you enjoyed literary subjects at school, but decided that you were more commercially minded than academic. Broadly, your preferences will direct you towards careers that are administrative. You will no doubt be involved with communications and probably the management of others as well. These careers may not have much in the way of a literary or creative content, but may have great variety and scope for expression in a practical way.

Organizational and Art

You are seeking a creative environment as well as responsibility for getting things done. You might enjoy working in a fast-paced, hectic job where the end result nevertheless has to be a superb performance.

Business and Words

Your own background might be literary and you might enjoy writing yourself. However, your greater interest is to combine your interest in books and ideas in business. Also, you might be drawn to a career where you are 'in the spotlight'. In this case, your career might be connected with communications.

Business and Art

These preferences almost always signify a desire to have a varied, enterprising career. You will enjoy a career that involves you with design or with the media. You like ideas and will seek opportunities for some original expression. You will probably be quick to spot something that is material, or an idea that will appeal to others. Often, you can arrange these things in a way that demonstrates the appeal of what you have discovered.

Part 4

Career Profiles

Career database

There are two ways of using these suggested profiles: first, working down the career list, stopping at those that appeal to you and checking out what characteristics are suggested, seeing if you have a similar or near match; and second, working down the characteristics, stopping at those occupations that have some resemblance to your own results.

Considerable caution, as well as intuition, is required to obtain the most from matching your characteristics to the profiles. These are some points to bear in mind:

- The fact that your own results do not match those suggested does not mean that the career will not suit you. The suggestions are only intended to give an indication of some of the most likely characteristics associated with that occupation. These are not the only possible ones.
- Where you do not have the characteristics suggested, but like the sound of the occupation, always ask yourself how your own characteristics might also be suitable. The main purpose of this exercise is to get you thinking for yourself about how you can use your potential most effectively. Different people with different characteristics may do the same job equally successfully.

- Where your characteristics in one area, say motivation, coincide with many possible occupations, use the aptitude and personality areas to narrow down the possibilities.
- Where you seem to be suited to one career because of your potential, say aptitudes, but to another career because of some other aspect of your potential, say personality, you are the only person who can decide what will suit you best.
- Two or more ticks against an occupation does not mean that each of these areas carries equal importance. For example, a manager might be good at visual, verbal and numerical reasoning, or only one of them.
- Where an occupation appears against which there are no ticks, this does not indicate that aptitude is unnecessary, but rather that none of the areas stands out as likely to be more important than the others.
- Ticks in the aptitudes area indicate where some potential is likely to be required. In relation to occupations that might require a degree as a starting point, potential is likely to be required at least at the level of 'above average'.

This book can only act as a guide and help to structure your thinking about your potential. Get further advice wherever you can, either from people who know you or from people who have expertise, such as careers counsellors.

Aptitude code		Personality code		Motivation code	
V	Visual	F	Factual	W	Words
N	Numerical	I	Imaginative	A	Art
Ve	Verbal	S	Spontaneous	P	Practical
S	Sequences	D	Deliberate	E	Experimenting
Sp	Spatial	A	Assertive	O	Organizing
3D	Three-D	P	Passive	B	Business
Sy	Systems	G	Group	S	Social
Vo	Vocabulary	So	Solitary		
Fi	Figurework				

Career	Aptitude									Personality								Motivation						
	V	N	Ve	S	Sp	3D	Sy	Vo	Fi	F	I	S	D	A	P	G	So	W	A	P	E	O	B	S
Accident assessor			✓		✓	✓			✓	✓			✓							✓				
Accountant		✓					✓		✓	✓			✓	✓								✓	✓	
Accounting technician		✓					✓		✓	✓			✓	✓								✓		
Actor			✓					✓		✓	✓							✓	✓					
Actuary	✓	✓		✓			✓		✓	✓			✓								✓	✓		
Acupuncturist	✓				✓					✓			✓		✓						✓			✓
Administrator							✓	✓	✓	✓			✓									✓		
Advertising copywriter			✓		✓			✓			✓							✓						
Advertising executive			✓	✓	✓			✓						✓		✓		✓					✓	
Aerobics instructor	✓								✓	✓		✓	✓	✓		✓		✓	✓					✓
Aeronautical engineer	✓	✓			✓	✓			✓	✓			✓		✓					✓	✓			
Aeronautical technician		✓				✓			✓	✓			✓		✓					✓	✓			
Agriculturalist	✓	✓			✓					✓			✓		✓					✓	✓			
Agricultural mechanic		✓			✓					✓			✓		✓		✓			✓				
Agricultural secretary							✓								✓			✓		✓				
Airline cabin staff								✓				✓				✓			✓	✓				
Air traffic controller	✓	✓							✓	✓			✓		✓		✓			✓	✓			✓
Ambulance crew		✓								✓			✓		✓		✓			✓				✓
Anaesthetist	✓	✓		✓					✓	✓			✓				✓				✓			✓
Animal keeper																	✓			✓				
Animal nurse										✓							✓			✓				
Anthropologist	✓		✓	✓													✓	✓	✓	✓				

	V	N	Ve	S	Sp	3D	Sy	Vo	Fi	F	I	S	D	A	P	G	So	W	A	P	E	O	B	S
Antique dealer					✓				✓	✓				✓					✓				✓	
Appliance repairer					✓	✓				✓					✓		✓							
Arborist					✓										✓		✓			✓				
Architect	✓	✓			✓	✓			✓		✓		✓	✓	✓		✓		✓	✓				
Architectural technician	✓				✓	✓			✓		✓		✓		✓		✓		✓					
Archivist			✓				✓	✓					✓					✓				✓		
Armed forces officer	✓	✓							✓	✓				✓		✓				✓			✓	✓
Armed forces personnel										✓						✓			✓	✓				✓
Aromatherapist	✓										✓	✓				✓								✓
Art dealer					✓						✓			✓	✓				✓					
Artist					✓						✓								✓				✓	
Art restorer					✓						✓		✓		✓		✓		✓		✓			
Art therapist					✓						✓				✓		✓	✓	✓					✓
Arts administrator	✓	✓					✓		✓	✓					✓	✓			✓			✓		
Astronaut	✓	✓					✓		✓	✓			✓		✓					✓	✓			
Astronomer	✓	✓							✓	✓			✓		✓						✓			
Auctioneer									✓	✓		✓		✓			✓						✓	
Audiology technician	✓					✓			✓	✓			✓		✓		✓				✓			
Auditor		✓		✓			✓			✓	✓				✓		✓					✓		
Author		✓		✓				✓							✓		✓	✓						
Automobile technician					✓	✓				✓							✓			✓				
Bacteriologist	✓	✓					✓			✓					✓		✓				✓			

	V	N	Ve	S	Sp	3D	Sy	Vo	Fi	F	I	S	D	A	P	G	So	W	A	P	E	O	B	S
Baggage handler																	✓			✓				
Baker												✓			✓		✓							
Ballet dancer					✓														✓					
Bank clerk		✓					✓		✓	✓	✓	✓	✓		✓				✓			✓		
Bank manager		✓					✓		✓	✓			✓	✓	✓	✓						✓	✓	
Bar person										✓	✓	✓			✓	✓		✓		✓				
Barrister		✓	✓					✓	✓		✓	✓		✓					✓				✓	
Beautician					✓							✓				✓								✓
Bicycle repairer						✓									✓		✓	✓						
Bilingual secretary		✓	✓				✓				✓						✓							
Biologist	✓	✓								✓							✓				✓			
Biomedical engineer		✓				✓				✓			✓		✓		✓			✓	✓			
Blacksmith/farrier																	✓			✓				
Boat builder					✓	✓									✓		✓		✓	✓				
Book binder					✓	✓									✓		✓		✓					
Book critic			✓					✓			✓	✓			✓		✓	✓						
Book illustrator											✓				✓		✓		✓					
Bookseller		✓											✓		✓		✓						✓	
Botanist	✓									✓							✓				✓			
Brewer										✓										✓	✓			
Bricklayer						✓							✓		✓					✓				
Broker		✓							✓	✓		✓		✓									✓	
Builder's merchant		✓							✓	✓												✓		

	V	N	Ve	S	Sp	3D	Sy	Vo	Fi	F	I	S	D	A	P	G	So	W	A	P	E	O	B	S
Building demolition expert				✓	✓								✓		✓		✓			✓				
Building inspector						✓			✓	✓			✓		✓		✓			✓		✓		
Building society assistant		✓					✓		✓	✓			✓		✓	✓					✓			
Building society manager		✓					✓		✓	✓			✓								✓	✓		
Building surveyor					✓				✓	✓			✓		✓		✓		✓	✓				
Bursar		✓							✓	✓			✓		✓						✓			
Bus driver															✓					✓				
Business consultant		✓		✓					✓	✓				✓									✓	
Buyer		✓			✓		✓		✓		✓		✓	✓					✓				✓	
Cabinet maker					✓						✓		✓		✓		✓		✓					
Camera repairer						✓					✓				✓		✓							
Car body designer					✓						✓	✓							✓					
Careers adviser														✓		✓								✓
Carpenter						✓					✓				✓		✓							
Cartographer					✓		✓						✓	✓	✓		✓		✓	✓				
Cartoon animator					✓						✓		✓	✓	✓		✓		✓					
Cashier		✓					✓			✓		✓	✓	✓	✓				✓			✓		
Caterer					✓				✓		✓	✓	✓		✓		✓		✓			✓	✓	
CD-ROM producer		✓			✓						✓						✓		✓					
Chef	✓				✓								✓		✓		✓							
Chemical technician	✓									✓			✓		✓		✓				✓			
Chemical technologist	✓									✓			✓				✓				✓			

	V	N	Ve	S	Sp	3D	Sy	Vo	Fi	F	I	S	D	A	P	G	So	W	A	P	E	O	B	S
Chemist	✓	✓							✓	✓			✓				✓				✓			
Chief executive	✓	✓	✓	✓			✓							✓								✓		
Child care worker								✓	✓						✓	✓	✓							✓
Chimney sweep																				✓				
Chiropodist	✓					✓			✓			✓	✓		✓		✓				✓			✓
Choreographer					✓						✓	✓							✓					
Cinema manager											✓		✓	✓		✓			✓			✓	✓	
Civil engineer	✓	✓				✓	✓		✓	✓			✓							✓	✓			
Civil servant	✓	✓	✓				✓	✓	✓		✓		✓		✓							✓		
Clerk										✓			✓		✓						✓			
Clinical psychologist	✓	✓	✓	✓			✓		✓	✓	✓				✓						✓			✓
Clown												✓			✓									
Club manager									✓		✓			✓	✓	✓	✓		✓				✓	
Coastguard															✓	✓				✓				
College admissions counsellor							✓						✓			✓						✓		✓
Comic illustrator					✓		✓			✓	✓			✓					✓					
Commercial account manager	✓	✓							✓		✓				✓	✓						✓	✓	
Community social worker															✓	✓						✓		✓
Community warden										✓					✓									✓
Company secretary	✓	✓					✓	✓	✓				✓		✓		✓	✓				✓		
Compositor	✓					✓					✓		✓				✓		✓					
Computer animator	✓	✓				✓					✓		✓						✓		✓			
Computer game designer	✓				✓	✓	✓				✓	✓			✓		✓		✓					

	V	N	Ve	S	Sp	3D	Sy	Vo	Fi	F	I	S	D	A	P	G	So	W	A	P	E	O	B	S
Computer hardware designer	✔	✔			✔	✔				✔			✔							✔	✔			
Computer systems analyst				✔									✔				✔				✔	✔		
Computer technician	✔				✔					✔			✔				✔			✔	✔			
Confectioner											✔			✔					✔					
Conference organizer												✔			✔	✔			✔			✔		
Conservation officer	✔												✔		✔		✔		✔		✔			
Copywriter			✔					✔			✔							✔						
Coroner	✔	✔								✔			✔		✔		✔	✔			✔	✔		
Cost accountant		✔					✔		✔	✔			✔											
Counsellor											✔	✔			✔	✔								✔
Courier												✔			✔		✔		✔					
Court reporter										✔			✔		✔		✔	✔		✔				
Crane operator														✔										
Criminologist	✔			✔									✔	✔				✔						
Cruise director										✔					✔	✔	✔	✔			✔		✔	
Cryptographer	✔			✔	✔		✔	✔				✔	✔		✔		✔	✔	✔					
Cultural anthropologist	✔		✔								✔					✔			✔					
Curator			✔		✔							✔	✔	✔	✔	✔	✔							
Currency trader		✔							✔	✔													✔	✔
Customer services manager									✔				✔	✔			✔					✔		✔
Customs officer									✔	✔			✔							✔		✔		
Dancer											✔	✔							✔					

Career	S	B	O	E	P	A	W	So	G	P	A	D	S	I	F	Fi	Vo	Sy	3D	Sp	S	Ve	N	V
Dance instructor	✓					✓			✓				✓	✓										✓
Deaf interpreter	✓									✓													✓	
Decorator						✓		✓						✓						✓				
Demonstrator		✓									✓		✓											
Dental assistant	✓			✓						✓		✓			✓									✓
Dental hygienist	✓			✓						✓		✓			✓									✓
Dental nurse	✓			✓						✓		✓			✓									✓
Dental technician				✓	✓							✓			✓				✓					✓
Dentist	✓			✓				✓	✓			✓			✓				✓	✓			✓	✓
Dermatologist				✓							✓	✓			✓									✓
Design engineer						✓		✓				✓		✓					✓				✓	
Designer				✓		✓		✓					✓	✓						✓				
Dietician										✓					✓				✓					✓
Director (media)		✓				✓	✓				✓			✓			✓				✓	✓		
Disc jockey						✓			✓				✓	✓				✓						✓
Dispensing optician		✓		✓				✓			✓	✓			✓			✓						
Display artist						✓				✓		✓	✓	✓						✓				
Diver					✓					✓		✓			✓				✓					
Doctor of medicine	✓			✓				✓		✓		✓	✓	✓	✓				✓				✓	✓
Drama teacher	✓						✓										✓							
Draughtsperson						✓		✓		✓									✓				✓	
Dresser (stage)						✓		✓		✓			✓	✓					✓	✓				
Dressmaker					✓	✓		✓		✓			✓	✓					✓	✓				

	V	N	Ve	S	Sp	3D	Sy	Vo	Fi	F	I	S	D	A	P	G	So	W	A	P	E	O	B	S
Driver													✓		✓		✓			✓				
Drug & alcohol counsellor											✓				✓									✓
Drycleaner										✓				✓									✓	
Ecologist	✓			✓							✓		✓		✓						✓			
Economist		✓	✓					✓		✓			✓									✓		
Editor		✓	✓				✓	✓			✓		✓		✓									
Editor (newspaper)			✓				✓	✓	✓		✓	✓		✓		✓							✓	
Editorial cartoonist			✓		✓						✓	✓							✓					
Educational psychologist	✓	✓	✓												✓		✓			✓	✓			✓
Electrical engineer		✓				✓				✓			✓		✓					✓	✓			
Electrician						✓				✓			✓				✓	✓		✓				
Electronics engineer		✓				✓				✓			✓				✓	✓			✓			
Elementary school teacher					✓		✓	✓	✓		✓		✓		✓		✓							✓
Embalmer					✓								✓		✓				✓					✓
Employment officer													✓		✓		✓		✓			✓		
Engineering pattern maker		✓				✓				✓			✓		✓				✓	✓				
Engineering technician		✓				✓				✓			✓		✓					✓				
English language teacher			✓					✓			✓	✓						✓						✓
Engraver					✓						✓	✓					✓		✓					
Entertainments officer											✓	✓							✓		✓			
Environmental health officer	✓									✓			✓				✓			✓	✓			
Equestrian															✓					✓				

	V	N	Ve	S	Sp	3D	Sy	Vo	Fi	F	I	S	D	A	P	G	So	W	A	P	E	O	B	S
Ergonomist		✓			✓	✓				✓					✓		✓		✓	✓	✓			
Estate agent					✓									✓								✓	✓	
Estate manager									✓				✓	✓		✓			✓	✓	✓	✓		
Exhibition organizer									✓			✓		✓		✓		✓				✓		
Explosives expert	✓			✓	✓		✓			✓			✓				✓		✓	✓	✓			
Farmer						✓																	✓	
Farm manager		✓				✓			✓	✓			✓	✓			✓		✓			✓		
Farm worker															✓		✓		✓					
Fashion buyer		✓			✓						✓	✓		✓				✓						✓
Fashion designer					✓						✓	✓			✓			✓						
Film projectionist						✓					✓				✓		✓	✓						
Film reviewer			✓		✓			✓			✓						✓	✓						
Financial analyst		✓					✓		✓	✓			✓		✓		✓					✓		
Financial controller		✓					✓		✓	✓			✓	✓								✓	✓	
Firefighter							✓			✓			✓				✓							
Fisheries officer													✓				✓		✓	✓				
Fisherman																	✓		✓	✓				
Fitter						✓									✓				✓	✓				
Flight attendant											✓	✓	✓		✓	✓	✓			✓				✓
Florist					✓						✓	✓			✓		✓	✓						
Flyman (theatre)					✓										✓				✓					
Food hygiene inspector	✓									✓			✓		✓						✓			

	V	N	Ve	S	Sp	3D	Sy	Vo	Fi	F	I	S	D	A	P	G	So	W	A	P	E	O	B	S
Food service worker																✓	✓			✓				
Foreign correspondent		✓	✓					✓			✓	✓					✓	✓						
Foreign language teacher		✓	✓					✓			✓	✓						✓						✓
Forensic pathologist	✓				✓	✓				✓			✓		✓		✓				✓			
Forensic psychologist	✓	✓		✓	✓			✓		✓			✓		✓		✓				✓			
Forensic scientist	✓	✓				✓				✓			✓		✓		✓				✓			
Forester																				✓				
Freelance writer			✓					✓			✓	✓		✓		✓		✓				✓	✓	
Fund raiser											✓		✓	✓									✓	
Funeral director													✓	✓							✓			
Furniture maker	✓				✓												✓		✓	✓				
Gamekeeper																✓				✓				
Gardener																			✓	✓				
Genealogist	✓						✓			✓			✓		✓		✓				✓			
Geneticist	✓	✓								✓			✓		✓		✓				✓			
Geochemist	✓	✓								✓			✓		✓		✓				✓			
Geologist	✓	✓		✓						✓			✓		✓		✓				✓			
Glassblower																	✓		✓	✓				
Glazier						✓								✓					✓	✓				
Golf professional											✓	✓				✓	✓		✓				✓	
Graphic designer					✓									✓										
Grocer									✓				✓	✓									✓	

	V	N	Ve	S	Sp	3D	Sy	Vo	Fi	F	I	S	D	A	P	G	So	W	A	P	E	O	B	S
Groundsperson															✓		✓			✓				
Guard										✓			✓				✓			✓				
Gunsmith				✓	✓	✓							✓		✓		✓		✓	✓				
Hairdresser					✓					✓	✓	✓				✓			✓					✓
Head teacher		✓	✓					✓	✓					✓		✓						✓		✓
Health services administrator							✓		✓	✓			✓									✓		
Health visitor	✓									✓			✓											✓
Heating engineer						✓								✓	✓		✓							
Historian								✓									✓	✓		✓				
Homeopath	✓		✓							✓			✓		✓		✓				✓			
Horologist													✓		✓					✓	✓			
Horticulturalist	✓	✓				✓				✓					✓		✓				✓			
Hospital physicist	✓	✓		✓		✓									✓		✓				✓			
Hospital porter													✓		✓						✓			
Hostel warden					✓									✓		✓				✓				
Hotel manager	✓								✓	✓			✓		✓	✓						✓	✓	✓
House parent	✓														✓	✓								✓
Housing manager							✓		✓					✓						✓				✓
Human resources manager		✓					✓	✓														✓	✓	✓
Hydrographic surveyor	✓					✓				✓			✓		✓		✓				✓			
Hydrologist	✓					✓				✓			✓				✓				✓			

	V	N	Ve	S	Sp	3D	Sy	Vo	Fi	F	I	S	D	A	P	G	So	W	A	P	E	O	B	S
Illustrator	✓				✓						✓		✓	✓			✓		✓					
Immunologist	✓	✓								✓			✓		✓						✓			
Importer/exporter		✓							✓					✓								✓	✓	
Industrial designer					✓						✓		✓						✓					
Industrial nurse	✓									✓			✓		✓						✓			✓
Industrial relations officer														✓									✓	✓
Information officer								✓			✓		✓	✓	✓	✓	✓	✓		✓				
Information scientist								✓		✓			✓		✓		✓	✓		✓	✓			
Instrument & control engineer		✓			✓					✓			✓	✓	✓						✓			
Instrument maker		✓				✓				✓			✓											
Insurance adjuster							✓		✓	✓			✓	✓								✓		
Insurance agent							✓		✓	✓							✓					✓		
Interior designer					✓						✓	✓							✓					
Interpreter			✓								✓	✓						✓						
Interviewer											✓			✓	✓		✓	✓						✓
Jewellery maker					✓						✓	✓			✓		✓		✓					
Jockey														✓			✓		✓	✓				
Joiner						✓						✓			✓					✓				
Journalist			✓					✓			✓		✓	✓			✓	✓						
Judge			✓	✓				✓					✓	✓			✓	✓						
Justices clerk																		✓			✓			

	V	N	Ve	S	Sp	3D	Sy	Vo	Fi	F	I	S	D	A	P	G	So	W	A	P	E	O	B	S
Laboratory technician	✓					✓				✓			✓		✓						✓			
Landscape architect	✓	✓			✓								✓		✓									
Language teacher			✓					✓		✓	✓	✓			✓		✓	✓	✓					✓
Lawyer			✓	✓				✓	✓	✓	✓		✓	✓				✓						
Legal executive	✓		✓				✓	✓	✓				✓	✓	✓									
Leisure centre staff												✓				✓						✓		
Liberal studies teacher	✓										✓	✓												✓
Librarian	✓						✓	✓			✓		✓		✓		✓	✓	✓	✓	✓			
Library assistant							✓	✓			✓		✓		✓		✓	✓				✓		
Lighthouse keeper															✓		✓	✓		✓		✓		
Lighting technician						✓				✓			✓		✓		✓		✓	✓				
Linguist			✓					✓			✓	✓				✓		✓						
Literary agent			✓					✓			✓		✓	✓				✓					✓	
Literary critic			✓					✓			✓	✓		✓				✓						
Lock keeper										✓					✓		✓			✓				
Locksmith		✓				✓				✓			✓		✓		✓			✓				
Locomotive engineer						✓				✓			✓		✓		✓			✓	✓			
Lorry driver																	✓			✓				
Machinist															✓		✓		✓	✓				
Maintenance technician										✓			✓		✓				✓	✓				
Maitre d'										✓	✓	✓		✓		✓			✓					
Make-up artist										✓	✓	✓							✓					

	V	N	Ve	S	Sp	3D	Sy	Vo	Fi		F	I	S	D	A	P	G	So	W	A	P	E	O	B	S
Management consultant		✓		✓							✓		✓	✓	✓		✓							✓	
Managing director		✓	✓	✓										✓	✓		✓							✓	✓
Marine biologist	✓								✓		✓			✓		✓						✓			
Market gardener								✓				✓		✓						✓	✓			✓	✓
Marketing manager		✓			✓				✓			✓		✓	✓					✓		✓		✓	
Market researcher		✓					✓					✓	✓	✓	✓							✓	✓		✓
Masseur/masseuse												✓	✓			✓				✓					
Materials scientist		✓			✓	✓					✓			✓							✓	✓			
Mathematician		✓			✓				✓		✓	✓	✓								✓	✓			
Mechanic						✓					✓			✓	✓	✓		✓			✓				
Mechanical engineer		✓				✓					✓			✓		✓	✓				✓	✓			
Medical illustrator					✓						✓	✓		✓	✓	✓		✓		✓			✓		
Medical records officer	✓						✓							✓		✓							✓		
Medical representative	✓										✓	✓	✓		✓							✓	✓		
Medical secretary	✓						✓		✓			✓		✓	✓	✓		✓					✓	✓	✓
Mental nurse	✓											✓	✓	✓	✓	✓		✓			✓	✓			✓
Merchandiser		✓							✓		✓	✓	✓		✓	✓				✓		✓			
Merchant seaman											✓			✓		✓					✓				
Metallurgist		✓				✓					✓			✓				✓				✓			
Meteorologist					✓						✓			✓		✓		✓				✓			
Microbiologist	✓	✓									✓			✓	✓			✓				✓	✓		
Midwife	✓												✓	✓	✓	✓	✓	✓			✓	✓		✓	
Milkman																					✓				

	V	N	Ve	S	Sp	3D	Sy	Vo	Fi	F	I	S	D	A	P	G	So	W	A	P	E	O	B	S
Miller																			✓	✓				
Milliner					✓							✓			✓		✓		✓	✓				
Miner													✓		✓	✓								
Minister of religion											✓			✓			✓							✓
Model (fashion)											✓	✓							✓					
Model maker					✓	✓					✓		✓		✓		✓		✓	✓				
Museum assistant											✓		✓		✓				✓		✓			
Musician											✓	✓		✓										
Music producer										✓		✓							✓				✓	
Music therapist											✓	✓			✓				✓					✓
Nanny										✓	✓	✓	✓		✓									✓
Nature conservancy warden	✓	✓								✓	✓		✓				✓			✓				
Navigating officer					✓		✓		✓	✓		✓			✓					✓	✓			
Negotiator									✓		✓			✓								✓		
Neurosurgeon	✓	✓		✓	✓	✓				✓			✓								✓			
Notary public			✓				✓	✓				✓	✓		✓		✓	✓						
Novelist			✓					✓										✓						
Nuclear physicist	✓	✓			✓	✓				✓	✓	✓	✓		✓						✓			
Nurse		✓								✓	✓	✓			✓						✓			✓
Nursery nurse												✓	✓		✓									✓
Nutritionist	✓									✓							✓				✓			

	V	N	Ve	S	Sp	3D	Sy	Vo	Fi	F	I	S	D	A	P	G	So	W	A	P	E	O	B	S
Obstetrician	✓	✓								✓			✓								✓			✓
Occupational psychologist	✓	✓								✓			✓	✓							✓		✓	✓
Occupational therapist			✓		✓	✓							✓		✓		✓							✓
Office cleaner													✓		✓		✓		✓	✓				
Office machinery mechanic		✓				✓							✓		✓		✓			✓				
Office manager		✓					✓	✓	✓	✓		✓	✓	✓			✓					✓	✓	
Oil rig worker						✓				✓	✓	✓			✓					✓				
Operational researcher	✓	✓		✓	✓		✓			✓			✓		✓		✓				✓			
Opthalmic optician	✓					✓				✓			✓		✓		✓				✓		✓	
Optician (dispensing)	✓					✓	✓			✓	✓	✓		✓							✓			
Organization & methods officer		✓		✓	✓				✓	✓			✓								✓			
Orthodontist	✓				✓	✓				✓			✓	✓	✓						✓	✓		✓
Orthoptist	✓				✓	✓				✓	✓		✓	✓	✓		✓				✓			
Osteopath					✓						✓		✓			✓					✓			
Outplacement consultant	✓							✓				✓	✓			✓	✓					✓	✓	✓
Panel beater						✓							✓				✓			✓				
Paramedic										✓			✓	✓							✓			✓
Patent agent	✓	✓		✓	✓	✓	✓	✓		✓			✓		✓		✓	✓		✓			✓	
Patent examiner	✓	✓		✓	✓	✓	✓	✓		✓			✓	✓				✓			✓			
Pathologist	✓	✓				✓				✓			✓		✓						✓			
Pattern cutter						✓													✓					
Personal trainer											✓		✓	✓										✓

	V	N	Ve	S	Sp	3D	Sy	Vo	Fi	F	I	S	D	A	P	G	So	W	A	P	E	O	B	S
Pharmacist	✓						✓			✓			✓	✓							✓	✓		
Pharmacologist	✓		✓	✓	✓	✓				✓			✓		✓		✓				✓			
Philosopher			✓	✓													✓	✓						
Photographer					✓		✓										✓		✓					
Photographic technician	✓				✓					✓		✓			✓		✓		✓	✓				
Physical education teacher	✓									✓		✓		✓	✓	✓	✓			✓				
Physicist	✓	✓			✓	✓				✓		✓	✓											✓
Physiotherapist					✓						✓	✓			✓		✓		✓		✓			✓
Piano teacher											✓	✓			✓		✓		✓		✓			✓
Piano tuner											✓	✓			✓				✓					
Picture framer					✓	✓					✓	✓					✓		✓	✓	✓			
Pilot (airplane)		✓			✓	✓			✓	✓	✓	✓	✓				✓			✓				
Pilot (coastal)					✓	✓			✓	✓	✓	✓	✓		✓		✓			✓				
Plasterer		✓			✓						✓	✓			✓	✓			✓					
Play leader										✓	✓	✓					✓							✓
Plumber		✓				✓				✓	✓	✓			✓		✓	✓		✓				
Poet			✓					✓		✓							✓							
Police dog handler				✓		✓								✓			✓			✓				
Police officer								✓					✓	✓		✓	✓	✓		✓			✓	✓
Political agent							✓	✓				✓		✓	✓								✓	✓
Politician			✓							✓													✓	
Pool and spa operator					✓						✓	✓			✓		✓		✓	✓				
Poster designer					✓	✓					✓	✓												

	V	N	Ve	S	Sp	3D	Sy	Vo	Fi	F	I	S	D	A	P	G	So	W	A	P	E	O	B	S
Postman/woman									✓						✓		✓							
Post office clerk							✓					✓	✓		✓		✓					✓		
Potter				✓	✓	✓																		
Press agent			✓							✓								✓						
Principal nursing officer	✓											✓	✓				✓			✓	✓			✓
Printer												✓	✓	✓	✓	✓		✓	✓	✓				✓
Prison officer									✓				✓	✓	✓									✓
Probation officer												✓	✓	✓	✓									✓
Producer (films)	✓	✓			✓			✓		✓	✓		✓	✓	✓	✓		✓	✓			✓	✓	
Production manager					✓					✓	✓	✓	✓	✓		✓								
Programmer	✓	✓			✓	✓			✓						✓		✓							
Property negotiator							✓			✓		✓	✓		✓		✓					✓	✓	
Prosthetics engineer	✓	✓								✓		✓	✓	✓						✓	✓			
Psychiatric social worker	✓						✓			✓	✓	✓		✓	✓	✓	✓	✓		✓				✓
Psychiatrist	✓	✓	✓							✓	✓	✓	✓	✓	✓	✓	✓	✓			✓			✓
Psychoanalyst	✓	✓	✓							✓	✓	✓		✓	✓	✓	✓	✓						✓
Psychologist	✓	✓	✓								✓	✓	✓		✓	✓	✓	✓		✓				✓
Psychotherapist	✓								✓	✓	✓	✓					✓		✓					
Publican										✓					✓				✓					
Publicity agent		✓	✓									✓	✓	✓				✓	✓				✓	
Public relations executive		✓	✓									✓	✓	✓				✓	✓				✓	
Publisher		✓	✓					✓				✓		✓				✓					✓	
Purchasing manager	✓			✓		✓	✓			✓			✓	✓		✓						✓	✓	

	V	N	Ve	S	Sp	3D	Sy	Vo	Fi	F	I	S	D	A	P	G	So	W	A	P	E	O	B	S
Purser		✓					✓		✓	✓			✓		✓					✓		✓		
Quality controller		✓				✓	✓		✓	✓			✓							✓	✓			
Quality inspector		✓				✓	✓		✓	✓			✓	✓			✓			✓	✓			
Quantity surveyor	✓	✓			✓	✓	✓		✓	✓			✓		✓		✓			✓		✓		
Racing car driver										✓		✓		✓	✓					✓				
Radiographer	✓	✓				✓				✓		✓	✓				✓			✓	✓			
Railway guard										✓			✓	✓	✓		✓			✓				
Rating valuation officer	✓	✓					✓		✓	✓			✓							✓		✓		
Receptionist											✓	✓			✓	✓		✓	✓					✓
Recording engineer		✓			✓					✓			✓		✓		✓		✓		✓			
Reflexologist	✓	✓									✓	✓			✓		✓				✓			✓
Remedial teacher											✓	✓			✓		✓							✓
Renovator					✓						✓	✓	✓	✓	✓		✓	✓	✓					
Reporter			✓					✓									✓		✓	✓				
Restorer					✓										✓	✓	✓							
Retail assistant									✓					✓		✓							✓	
Retail manager									✓		✓	✓					✓					✓	✓	
Roofer						✓									✓				✓					
Saddler					✓					✓					✓		✓			✓				
Sailor												✓			✓					✓				

	V	N	Ve	S	Sp	3D	Sy	Vo	Fi	F	I	S	D	A	P	G	So	W	A	P	E	O	B	
Sales executive									✓			✓	✓	✓	✓								✓	
Sales manager		✓		✓			✓	✓	✓					✓	✓								✓	
Salesperson									✓			✓		✓	✓	✓							✓	
Sales trainer			✓	✓					✓		✓	✓		✓									✓	✓
Science teacher	✓	✓							✓	✓		✓			✓		✓	✓			✓			✓
Science writer	✓	✓						✓			✓	✓			✓		✓				✓	✓		
Scientific instrument maker	✓					✓				✓			✓		✓		✓				✓			
Scriptwriter								✓			✓	✓		✓			✓	✓		✓				
Sculptor			✓		✓						✓	✓							✓					
Secretary/PA							✓		✓	✓	✓		✓		✓		✓	✓	✓					
Securities analyst		✓					✓		✓	✓			✓		✓		✓				✓			
Security officer													✓		✓					✓				
Session musician											✓	✓			✓				✓					
Set designer					✓	✓					✓	✓			✓		✓		✓					
Shepherd										✓			✓				✓			✓				
Shipping & forwarding officer		✓					✓		✓	✓			✓									✓		
Shop fitter						✓									✓				✓	✓				
Sign writer					✓						✓		✓		✓		✓		✓					
Silversmith					✓					✓	✓		✓		✓		✓		✓					
Social scientist	✓										✓		✓					✓			✓		✓	✓
Social worker											✓			✓									✓	✓
Soldier										✓		✓			✓					✓				
Solicitor			✓				✓	✓	✓		✓		✓		✓			✓						

	V	N	Ve	S	Sp	3D	Sy	Vo	Fi	F	I	S	D	A	P	G	So	W	A	P	E	O	B	S
Sound engineer		✔								✔			✔				✔		✔		✔			
Space salesperson											✔	✔			✔		✔						✔	
Speech therapist						✔					✔	✔		✔			✔							✔
Sports coach	✔											✔		✔		✔				✔				✔
Sports official (referee)												✔								✔				
Stage hand					✔						✔	✔			✔		✔		✔					
Stage manager				✔				✔			✔	✔		✔	✔		✔		✔				✔	
Statistician		✔							✔	✔		✔	✔	✔	✔		✔				✔	✔		
Stockbroker		✔							✔	✔			✔		✔		✔					✔	✔	
Stock controller		✔					✔		✔	✔					✔		✔					✔		
Stone mason					✔						✔	✔							✔					
Studio assistant											✔	✔							✔	✔				
Stunt performer											✔	✔		✔										
Surgeon	✔	✔		✔	✔	✔				✔	✔	✔	✔		✔		✔				✔			
Surveyor		✔			✔					✔	✔		✔		✔		✔			✔		✔		
Systems analyst		✔			✔		✔			✔		✔					✔				✔	✔		
Tailor					✔										✔				✔					
Taxidermist					✔								✔		✔	✔			✔					
Taxi driver							✔		✔						✔									
Tax inspector							✔			✔			✔		✔							✔		
Teacher	✔	✔	✔		✔							✔					✔							✔
Teacher of art/craft		✔	✔																✔					✔

	V	N	Ve	S	Sp	3D	Sy	Vo	Fi		F	I	S	D	A	P	G	So		W	A	P	E	O	B	S
Teacher of handicapped	✓	✓														✓		✓								✓
Technical illustrator					✓	✓						✓		✓		✓		✓			✓		✓			
Technical representative						✓		✓			✓		✓		✓			✓				✓	✓		✓	
Technical writer						✓						✓		✓		✓		✓			✓		✓			
Telecommunications engineer		✓									✓			✓		✓		✓		✓			✓			
Telephonist												✓	✓			✓		✓				✓				✓
Television engineer						✓					✓			✓		✓		✓					✓			
Television production assistant												✓	✓			✓					✓	✓				
Thatcher				✓								✓		✓		✓		✓								
Theatre administrator	✓	✓					✓		✓			✓		✓			✓				✓			✓		
Tiler				✓	✓									✓		✓		✓								
Tool maker					✓	✓					✓	✓		✓		✓		✓				✓				
Toy maker					✓							✓		✓		✓		✓			✓	✓				
Tracer						✓								✓		✓		✓			✓					
Traffic warden			✓								✓	✓		✓		✓		✓		✓		✓				
Train driver			✓								✓	✓	✓			✓				✓		✓				
Training officer						✓							✓		✓	✓		✓			✓		✓			✓
Translator							✓							✓												
Transport manager									✓		✓	✓		✓		✓		✓			✓	✓				
Travel agent							✓																	✓	✓	
Truck driver													✓		✓							✓				
Turf accountant									✓		✓							✓						✓		

	V	N	Ve	S	Sp	3D	Sy	Vo	Fi	F	I	S	D	A	P	G	So	W	A	P	E	O	B	S
Umpire		✓							✓	✓				✓			✓			✓				✓
Underwriter		✓					✓		✓				✓		✓							✓		
Union negotiator													✓	✓									✓	
Upholsterer				✓											✓		✓		✓					
Urban planner	✓					✓	✓				✓	✓	✓		✓				✓			✓		
Veterinary nurse	✓									✓			✓		✓					✓				
Veterinary surgeon		✓			✓	✓				✓			✓							✓	✓			
Vision mixer						✓					✓		✓		✓				✓		✓			
Vocational counsellor				✓				✓			✓				✓									✓
Waiter/waitress											✓	✓	✓		✓				✓					✓
Watch repairer						✓					✓		✓		✓		✓			✓				
Welder						✓				✓	✓	✓					✓		✓	✓				
Window dresser					✓						✓		✓		✓	✓								
Word processor operator	✓			✓			✓						✓		✓			✓						
Work study officer							✓			✓	✓	✓		✓						✓		✓		
Writer			✓					✓										✓						
Youth worker											✓				✓		✓							✓
Zoo keeper	✓				✓												✓		✓		✓			
Zoologist	✓	✓								✓	✓	✓			✓		✓				✓			

Further reading from Kogan Page

Other best-selling books by Jim Barrett

The Aptitude Test Workbook, Jim Barrett, 2003
Career, Aptitude and Selection Tests, Jim Barrett, 1998
How to Pass Advanced Aptitude Tests, Jim Barrett, 2002
Test Your Own Aptitude, 3rd edn, Jim Barrett and Geoff Williams, 2003
'Will help you to pinpoint your potential and suitability for a particular career.' – *The Weekly Telegraph*

Other titles in the testing series

The Advanced Numeracy Test Workbook, Mike Bryon, 2003
How to Master Personality Questionnaires, 2nd edn, Mark Parkinson, 2000
How to Master Psychometric Tests, 2nd edn, Mark Parkinson, 2000
How to Pass Advanced Numeracy Tests, Mike Bryon, 2002

How to Pass Computer Selection Tests, Sanjay Modha, 1994

How to Pass Graduate Psychometric Tests, 2nd edn, Mike Bryon, 2001

How to Pass Graduate Recruitment Tests, Mike Bryon, 1994

How to Pass Numeracy Tests, 2nd edn, Harry Tolley and Ken Thomas, 2000

How to Pass Professional-level Psychometric Tests, Sam Al-Jajjoka, 2001

How to Pass Selection Tests, 2nd edn, Mike Bryon and Sanjay Modha, 1998

How to Pass Technical Selection Tests, Mike Bryon and Sanjay Modha, 1993

How to Pass the Civil Service Qualifying Tests, 2nd edn, Mike Bryon, 2003

How to Pass Verbal Reasoning Tests, Harry Tolley and Ken Thomas, 2000

How to Succeed at an Assessment Centre, Harry Tolley and Bob Wood, 2001

IQ and Psychometric Tests, Philip Carter, 2004

Test Your Creative Thinking, Lloyd King, 2003

Test Your IQ, Ken Russell and Philip Carter, 2000

The Times Book of IQ Tests – Book Four, Ken Russell and Philip Carter, 2004

The Times Book of IQ Tests – Book Three, Ken Russell and Philip Carter, 2003

The Times Book of IQ Tests – Book Two, Ken Russell and Philip Carter, 2002

The Times Book of IQ Tests – Book One, Ken Russell and Philip Carter, 2001

CD ROM

The Times Testing Series – Psychometric Tests, Volume 1, 2002

The Times Testing Series – Test Your Aptitude, Volume 1,
   2002
The Times Testing Series – Test Your IQ, Volume 1, 2002

The above titles are available from all good bookshops. For
further information, please contact the publisher at the
following address:

Kogan Page Limited
120 Pentonville Road
London N1 9JN
Tel: 020 7278 0433
Fax: 020 7837 6348
www.kogan-page.co.uk

THE ✥ TIMES

Published by Kogan Page Interactive, The Times Testing Series is an exciting new range of interactive CD ROMs that will provide invaluable practice tests for job applicants and for those seeking a brain-stretching challenge.

Each CD ROM features:

- hundreds of unique interactive questions
- instant scoring with feedback and analysis
- hours of practice and fun
- questions devised by top UK MENSA puzzle editors and test experts
- against-the-clock, real test conditions
- a program that allows users to create their own tests

Psychometric Tests
Volume 1

Psychometric Tests Volume 1 provides essential practice for any job applicant who has to face a selection test.

With this CD ROM users will be able to:

- practise on tests based on those used by top employers
- learn how to tackle different types of questions
- experience real test conditions
- receive instant results and invaluable feedback

THE ⚜ TIMES

Test Your IQ
Volume 1

This interactive CD ROM contains hundreds of questions just like those used in job selection IQ tests. *Test Your IQ* Volume 1 enables users to:

- practise for hours and achieve improved scores

- score against their friends

- develop their vocabulary and powers of logic

- practise on randomly selected tests every time

Test Your Aptitude
Volume 1

By working through the tests contained in this interactive CD ROM users will get a clear insight into what really makes them tick and the sort of job that would suit them best. *Test Your Aptitude* Volume 1 will reveal to users:

- what really motivates them

- which career best suits their personality

- their strengths and weaknesses

- how they will perform in selection tests

Available from all good bookshops, software outlets and the Kogan Page Web site. To obtain further information, please contact the publisher at the address below:

Kogan Page Ltd
120 Pentonville Road
London N1 9JN
Tel: 020 7278 0433
Fax: 020 7837 6348

www.kogan-page.co.uk